*Prai*

# Take the Stone Out of the Shoe

A Must-Have Guide to Understanding, Supporting, and Correcting Dyslexia, Learning, and Attention Challenges

*"Take the Stone Out of the Shoe* offers a clear, comprehensive, and much-needed road map of learning challenges and thoughtful remediation strategies to the parents of students who are struggling in school and/or who have complex learning profiles.

It is also a go-to resource for SLPs, OTs, and other professionals who often find themselves in the role of "translating" both the meaning and the academic and emotional impacts of diagnoses ranging from simple to complex learning challenges to caregivers.

The book's overarching and essential message that "It's going to be okay" is supported by numerous real-life examples of students who have struggled and ultimately succeeded. The simple, direct, and conversational tone in which Jill Stowell distills and communicates an impressive range of evidence-based information is designed to reassure and support caregivers in understanding and effectively advocating for their children. Stowell guides parents in understanding the key differences between (and potential intersections of) issues including sensory integration, visual and auditory processing challenges, dyslexia, ADHD, and executive function challenges. Her section on executive function includes the crucial message that the goal of interventions should be to support self-regulation on the part of students (a message she succinctly summarizes with the question, "Are you building or being their executive function?").

With its compassion, clarity, and thorough overview of learning challenges, Take the Stone Out of the Shoe fills a gap in the current literature–which tends to be either aimed at professionals, or aimed at addressing one specific challenge in depth–offering parents and students both hope and proven strategies for supporting understanding, success, and self-empowerment."

–Sarah Ward, M.S., CCC/SLP, Speech and Language Pathologist, Co-Director of Cognitive Connections, LLP, Co-Author of the 360 Thinking Executive Function Program

"Take the Stone out of the Shoe is a standout in the field of addressing learning challenges! As a Certified Trainer in the Collaborative Problem Solving®(MGH) approach, as well as other forms of intervention meant for children with chronic challenging behavior, I found Jill's book to be an incredibly valuable guide for parents.

Not only does she lay out a clear and user-friendly understanding of the many possible challenges that could be preventing a child from achieving their full potential within traditional learning systems, but also offers tangible hope in the form of guidance where it comes to identifying and applying targeted interventions that lead to results. She speaks not only from knowledge, but from a wealth of experience running the Stowell Learning Center, in a manner that opens welcoming arms to parents as partners in their child's education, and in working to "Take the Stone out of the Shoe" that may be preventing their progress."

–Doris Bowman, M.S., Advanced Certified Trauma Practitioner, Certified Collaborative Problem Solving® (MGH) Trainer, Certified HeartMath Trainer

"Jill Stowell is not only a colleague in this field but has been a mentor to me. As a cognitive consultant specializing in helping people find neuroplastic interventions I was thrilled to learn about her centers that have so many of these wonderful methods under one roof that I could refer families to.

Her first book, which I was introduced to in 2015, reaffirmed to me that we had to look at brain function and brain development to understand the origin of learning difficulties.

In her current book Jill organizes it into 3 sections. Why someone may be struggling, some strategies to support struggling learners (until their abilities can be improved through neuroplastic work and very specific skill training) and specifically about what she offers at her centers and why. There are stories of real students of different ages and abilities that many families will relate to. As well, she explains the science behind the origin of many learning difficulties and how the field of neuroscience has helped us learn how to resolve them. This book provides valuable information to many families looking for solutions."

–Alexandra Dunnison, M.ED.,Cognitive Consultant

"As a psychotherapist specializing with children and their families and as a Parent Effectiveness Training (PET) instructor for 30 years, I see the incredible value of this book. Learning challenges potentially can create longterm emotional and psychological challenges for children throughout their childhood and far into adulthood. These difficulties also take a toll on families creating power struggles and fights if not dealt with, with tools, support and understanding rather than frustrations, disappointments and punishments.

This well thought out book includes a section that offers support and understanding of the child's perspective and parents concerns.

There are examples and personal experiences in the book to make the read clear and accessible. Most will see glimpses, if not more than a glimpse, of their situation. There are names to the challenges and red flags to look for.

The second section gives strategies of ways to help. I read so many great ideas here–very practical strategies, ideas of things to try to help your child and reduce the stress in your home.

And lastly in the third section, you will find the science and evidence behind the challenges and solutions. This will provide you with the hope you need to enable your child to grow, develop and blossom to their full potential.

I enjoyed reading this book so much. Kudos to Jill Stowell and thanks for sharing her great knowledge and long time experience in this field of learning challenges.

It's a real gift to parents, children and professionals."
—Stephanie R. Bien, LMFT, LPCC, Founder of
Insight to Teen Culture

"Parents help shape the most complex organ in the universe–the human mind. But how much do any of us really know about our child's unique needs, strengths and challenges based on their complex sensory and brain systems? Brains aren't just born, they're built. And experience is the architect. Over the last few decades, we've made tremendous strides in neuroscience, child development and learning.

Jill Stowell, in her new book *Take the Stone Out of the Shoe* does a wonderful job at helping parents make sense of the very complex, brain-based challenges that can negatively impact a child's ability to learn, regulate and thrive.

I absolutely loved all the tangible activities and tools that parents can use immediately to build skills into their child's complex sensory brain systems. This is a 'must have' book for all parents who are raising a child with learning challenges."

—Allison Davis-Maxon, ED, Author, Speaker, Consultant in Child Welfare, Trauma, Attachment and Adoption/Permanency

"I am grateful for trailblazers like Jill Stowell who are helping to illuminate the significance of phonological awareness and auditory processing abilities to not only speech and language development, but to future academic success.

As a pediatric Speech-Language Pathologist with a special interest in foundational learning readiness, I am keenly aware that poor or delayed early speech and language development quite often leads to literacy challenges. Research has proven it. The good news is that this can be avoided with early detection and corrected with the right interventions.

Jill Stowell's expertise in the area of learning challenges and how to remediate them is remarkable, and she is a phenomenal resource for me professionally. "Take the Stone Out of the Shoe" is a must read for parents, educators, and even therapists, who work and live with children with learning differences.

Thank you, Jill, for providing this easy to read, and very relatable work."

–Stacy Payne, M.S., CCC-SLP, CLE, Pediatric Speech-Language Pathologist, ADHD – Certified Rehabilitative Services Provider, Executive Director, Bright Beginnings Pediatric Services

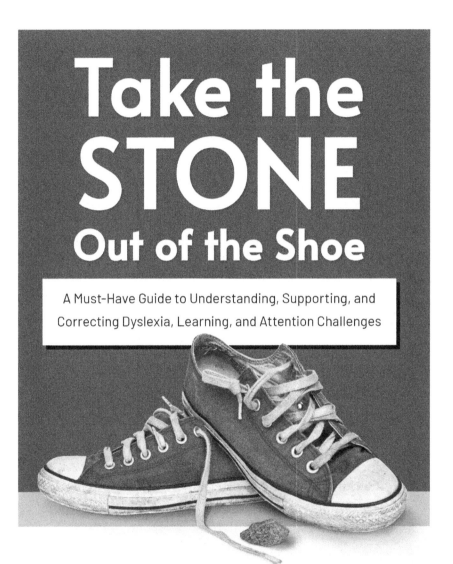

# Take the STONE Out of the Shoe

A Must-Have Guide to Understanding, Supporting, and Correcting Dyslexia, Learning, and Attention Challenges

## Jill Stowell

**#1 Bestselling Author:** *At Wit's End: A Parent's Guide to Ending the Struggle, Tears, and Turmoil of Learning Disabilities*

Copyright © 2021 Green Dot Press. All rights reserved. No part of this publication may be reproduced, stored in a retrieval system or transmitted in any form or by any means–electronic, mechanical, photocopy, recording or any other, except for brief quotations in printed reviews or articles.

Published by Green Dot Press

ISBN: 978-0-9989356-4-5

Printed in the United States

Book Cover Design by Christy Stowell
Interior Design and Typesetting by Lyn Adelstein

*Dedication*

This book is dedicated to every student who has come through the doors of Stowell Learning Center. Each of you has taught us something of incredible value that has impacted yet another student.

JILL STOWELL

## CONTENTS

## PART ONE: SMART BUT STRUGGLING WHAT DOES IT MEAN?

Introduction ..... 15

**1 Parents, You're Not Alone** ..... **21**
I Hate Feeling Crazy! ..... 21
Frightened for My Child ..... 23
"I Want My Son to Love School Again" ..... 24
Why Isn't the School Helping My Child? ..... 26
Why Does the School Say He's Fine When He's Failing Two Classes and Barely Passing the Rest? ..... 28
Did I Waste Time and Money on Therapy? ..... 30
"I Don't Want My Son Accommodated!" ..... 32

**2 I Wish My Parents And Teachers Understood How I Feel** ..... **35**
Mom, Am I Dumb? ..... 35
I'm Not a Reading Person ..... 36
I Can't Read a Thing, but My Teacher Thinks I'm a Reader! –*Dyslexic Second Grader* ..... 38
This Is So Boring! ..... 40
Learning Differences Don't Really Make Me Different! ..... 42
What if "Try Harder" Isn't the Answer? ..... 43

### 3  Understanding the Problem Beneath the Problem  47

The Skills Behind School Success: The Learning Skills Continuum  47

The Learning Skills Continuum Approach to Permanently Changing Learning and Attention Challenges  51

Does Your Child Have the Right Tools for the Job?  51

What Does It Really Mean When the School Says Your Struggling Student Doesn't Have a Learning Disability?  53

5 Reasons Why Your Child's Attention Problem Might NOT be ADHD  54

Dyslexia or ADHD?  59

### 4  What Do Challenges With Core Learning Skills Look LIke?  63

Challenges at the Core Learning Skills Level  63

Why Is Change So Hard?  64

Why Does My Child Act This Way?  How retained reflexes impact behavior and learning  66

I'm Ambidextrous! Isn't That Cool?  68

Tippy Toes and Learning Challenges  69

Fright, Fight, or Flight  71

Got Rhythm?
Rhythm and timing may be a factor in reading, attention, and learning problems  72

I'm Not Being a Wild Child on Purpose!  75

Understanding Students with Sensory
Processing Disorder (SPD)     76

## 5  What Do Challenges With Processing Skills Look Like?     79

Challenges at the Processing Skills Level     79

Auditory Processing Problems Are Like
Listening Underwater     80

Why Isn't Everybody Talking about Auditory
Processing?     81

The Listening–Learning Connection     84

The Listening–Emotional/Social Connection     87

Agh! My Teacher Talks Too Fast!
The impact of slow processing speed     88

"I Don't Get It. What Do You Mean?"
A look at comprehension challenges     89

HAPPY HOLIDAYS Form, Johnny
The impact of visual processing challenges     91

## 6  What Do Challenges With Executive Function Look Like?     95

Challenges with Executive Function     95

Is Poor Executive Function Getting Your Child in Trouble?     96

HELP! My Kid Is Driving Me Crazy Because…     96

ADHD–I'm Not Losing Focus on Purpose!     99

Multitasking or Scattered and Unfocused?
Is social media helping or hurting attention and executive function?     100

| | | |
|---|---|---|
| **7** | **Recognizing Challenges With Dyslexia, Dysgraphia, Dyscalculia, and Basic Academics** | **103** |
| | Is My Child Dyslexic? | 103 |
| | What Do Dyslexic Spelling Challenges Look Like? | 107 |
| | Dysgraphia Basics | 108 |
| | Why Do Students Struggle with Math? | 110 |
| **8** | **Quick Screening Tools** | **113** |
| | At-A-Glance Dyslexia Screener | 113 |
| | Quick Learning Disability Screening Tool | 115 |
| | Quick Auditory Processing Screening Tool | 117 |

## PART TWO: SIMPLE STRATEGIES FOR SUPPORTING STRUGGLING STUDENTS

| | | |
|---|---|---|
| | Introduction | 119 |
| **9** | **General Guidelines** | **121** |
| | Downtime Matters | 121 |
| | Lessons from Dad | 122 |
| | Brain Break Activities to Get Unstuck, Refocused, and Restarted | 124 |
| | Laughter: A Good Attitude Adjuster! | 127 |
| | 5 Tips for Empowering Kids and Building Self-Esteem | 129 |
| | Is Retention Ever a Good Idea? | 131 |

Food for Thought: Help Your Child Eat
for Success                                              134

Sleep Improves Memory, Learning, and
Emotional Regulation                                     137

Don't Tell Me to Try Harder                              138

Ask for More of the Good Stuff                           140

3 Simple Ways To Control Stress and
Screen Fatigue                                           141

## 10 Attention and Focus                                145

Child's Play Develops Attention                          145

Balance, the Foundation of Attention Training
                                                         146

5 Steps to Developing Impulse Control                    147

The Brain on ADHD
Flowcharts to the Rescue                                 149

Simple Focus Strategies                                  153

## 11 Executive Function and Organization
                                                         157

The Right Amount Of Control/Personal CEO  157

Are You Building or *Being* Their Executive
Function?                                                158

Develop Visualization as a Comprehension
and Memory Tool                                          160

Steps to Helping Children and Teens Develop
Executive Function and Problem-Solving Skills
                                                         160

7 Easy Organizational Strategies to Help
Students Start the School Year Right　164

Getting Homework Put Away and Turned In:
A Strategy for Creating New Habits　165

Metacognition: The Art of Self-Talk　166

## 12  Behavior And Social Skills　169

Surviving the Fireworks (And Loud
Situations) With Your Sensitive Child　169

Everyone Needs a Hula Hoop! Helping
Children Understand Social Space　171

What Every Parent Wants! Building your
child's confidence and self-esteem　172

Harness the Power of Words to Improve
Learning and Self-Esteem　174

Calming Back-to-School Jitters　175

## 13  Dyslexia, Reading, and Spelling　179

Accommodations and Modifications to
Support Dyslexic Students at School and
with Homework　179

Increase Decoding Fluency and Visual
Attention for Reading　184

Neurological Impress Reading to increase
reading accuracy and attention to meaning　185

Integrate the Brain for Reading and Writing　186

Classroom/Homework Spelling Tips and
Accommodations for Supporting Dyslexic
Students　187

## 14 Dysgraphia And Writing — 191

Is Handwriting Important? — 191
Alphabet 8s with weights — 193
Handwriting Without Tears Paper Produces Improved Writing — 195
5-Minute Power Writing Strategy — 196
Proofreading Strategy–COPS — 197

## 15 Comprehension And Memory — 199

Comprehension and Memory Strategies — 199
Concept Diagramming for Comprehension and Test Study — 200

## 16 Dyscalculia And Math — 203

Number Line — 203
Math Dialoguing Technique — 204
Dealing with Those Dreaded Word Problems — 204
Math Triangles (+ − × ÷ Facts) — 207
Memory Grid for Tough Multiplication Facts — 209

# PART THREE: REAL SOLUTIONS AND THE SCIENCE BEHIND THEM

Introduction — 213

## 17 What Does It Take To Permanently Correct A Learning Challenge? — 215

Identifying the Lagging Underlying Skills    215
Targeted Plan and Training    216
The Importance of Frequency and Intensity    217
Time    218
Programming    219

## 18 Music-Based Auditory Training    221

Sound Frequencies    221
Auditory Zoom    224
Neurological Connections and Sound Therapy/Auditory Training    226
The Listening Program (TLP) and inTime    227
Integrated Listening Systems (iLs)    229
Combining Listening and Movement    231
Safe and Sound Protocol (SSP)    232

## 19 Auditory Stimulation And Training    235

Passive Auditory Training    236
Auditory Feedback Loop    237
Feeding the Right Ear-Left Brain    238
Reading on the Wrong Side of the Brain    239
Audio-Vocal Training    240
Auditory Stimulation and Training–Reading and Spelling (AST-R/S)    241
Auditory Stimulation and Training–Comprehension (AST-C)    243

## 20 Reflex Integration and Movement Development — 249

   Exercise and Learning — 251
   Core Learning Skills Training (CLS) — 253
   Learning Reflexes — 254
   Additional Skill Areas — 263
   Quantum Reflex Integration (QRI) — 268
   QRI Outcomes with ADHD — 272

## 21 Cognitive Processing Skills Training — 277

   Attention, Memory, and Processing Skills (AMPS) — 280
   Processing and Cognitive Enhancement (PACE) — 281
   Attention Process Training (APT) — 282
   Perception Attention Therapy (PATH Therapy) — 282

## 22 Principles For Enhancing Attention, Behavior, and Executive Function — 285

   A Shift in Perspective — 285
   Problem Solve Together — 289
   The Dopamine Reward — 291
   Inner Language — 292
   Metacognition — 294
   Build the Critical Underlying Skills — 295

**23  Putting It All Together                      299**

**24  It's Time To Take The Stone Out Of
     The Shoe                                      303**

| | |
|---|---|
| Acknowledgements | 305 |
| Bibliography | 307 |
| About the Author | 313 |
| Index | 315 |

# TAKE THE STONE OUT OF THE SHOE

"No matter what it looks like, most people—parents, children, teens, adults—want to do well and are doing the best they can. When they struggle, it's not about not caring, or lack of motivation or laziness, it's because something is getting in the way. Once we really identify what that is, things can change."

–Jill Stowell

JILL STOWELL

# TAKE THE STONE OUT OF THE SHOE

*Preface*

I have always loved the population of students who fall under that learning disability umbrella–bright, creative, clever and so misunderstood and underserved–or perhaps mis-served because their struggles don't seem to make sense with their abilities. I can't help but smile when I think of these students–current and past. What a privilege it's been to work with them for my entire adult life.

There is nothing about struggling and neurodiverse students that needs to be "fixed." There is, however, much to be understood and redefined. Greater ease and enjoyment in learning is possible. It's time to update our approach to learning and attention challenges.

I wrote my first book, "At Wit's End, A Parent's Guide to Ending the Struggle, Tears, and Turmoil of Learning Disabilities" for the multitude of parents who told me that they were at their wit's end. I wanted them to understand the enigma of a bright but struggling student and what could be done to change that permanently. I have been so happy to hear how much the new understanding of learning and attention challenges has helped families.

"Take the Stone Out of the Shoe" was written in response to readers asking for more–for practical techniques that they could use immediately at home and school to support their struggling students, and for the research behind the new paradigm that the challenges associated with dyslexia, auditory processing disorders, and learning disabilities can be permanently eliminated.

I wrote this book to be a quick, easy read for all of you busy parents and teachers. You can read straight through or pick and choose what's relevant to you today. You'll find science and tools and most all, hope for your unique, amazing, struggling student.

Enjoy!
Jill Stowell
December 8, 2021

## Part 1: Smart but Struggling What Does It Mean?

### *Introduction*

**Just Call Me "Braben!"**

We had an adorable eight-year-old student named Braden. He was so dyslexic when we met him that after repeatedly reversing the *d* in his name, he told his teacher, "Just call me Braben!"

I had to laugh when I heard that because this young boy was so delightful and good-natured. But on further reflection, this is the very last thing that I want for our dyslexic students: to have to spend their life finding ways to get around their reading and writing challenges.

**Take the Stone Out of the Shoe!**

Imagine that you are a really talented soccer player, but you have a stone in your shoe. Your coach takes you aside and gives you special lessons–special techniques–for running with a stone in your shoe. Then you go back to the game. Even though you are very talented and motivated and you've had those special lessons for running with a stone in your shoe, playing soccer is still going to be harder for you than for your teammates.

> **Wouldn't it make more sense
> to take the stone out of the shoe?**

## What Does It Mean When Bright Students Struggle?

I once worked with a young man who was so dyslexic that he couldn't recognize his middle name in print. But he was also so smart that he dated a reading specialist for several months and she never knew he couldn't read!

Smart children and adults who struggle academically are often pegged as lazy or unmotivated. That couldn't be further from the truth.

Not only do they have to put out much more effort, time, and energy to complete tasks than their equally or less intelligent peers, but they often funnel considerable time, energy, and creativity into hiding their learning challenges.

While dating the reading teacher, Tony would go to whatever restaurant he wanted to take her to, get a menu, and take it home. His mom would read it to him so he could be prepared with what he wanted to order. Then he would pretend to read through the menu on his date and order his pre-selected item. Pretty smart, huh? So why couldn't he read?

Innate intelligence is certainly a factor in academic success, but having a high IQ doesn't automatically ensure it. Equally important are the underlying learning/processing skills that support efficient learning.

These are skills such as the following:
- Body awareness and control
- Auditory and visual processing that allow the student to get accurate and complete information to think with

# TAKE THE STONE OUT OF THE SHOE

- Memory, attention, and processing speed that allow them to get, hold onto, think about, and respond to information quickly
- Spatial orientation and organization that allow students to discriminate between letters and words that look similar, understand how math is laid out on the page, and see the organization in textbooks and planners
- Language processing and comprehension
- Reasoning, problem-solving, and higher-level organization

Students who have weaknesses in one or more of these areas often have to work harder and longer than their peers in school. If there are several areas of weakness or one or two areas that are very weak, the student may end up with real challenges with reading, spelling, writing, and/or math.

**This doesn't mean they're not smart. It means that key underlying learning skills are not supporting them well enough.**

Important research starting as far back as the 1950s and 1970s showed us that underlying skills can be developed so that smart but struggling students can stop struggling. Brain plasticity research has begun to reveal the amazing capacity of the brain to rewire itself for more efficient learning through specific and targeted training.[1]

If you have a smart but struggling learner in your family (child or adult), chances are that the challenges can be dramatically improved or completely and permanently corrected.

## What You'll Find in This Book

If you are the parent of a struggling student, you will find that you are not alone and that your instincts about your child are probably right on target.

You'll gain insights about what your child might be *feeling* as a struggling student, and an understanding of various types of learning challenges and the underlying processing skills at the root of those struggles.

A variety of hands-on, use-them-today strategies are included in this book to help parents avoid homework battles and support their struggling learners.

Teachers will find classroom strategies that will help them navigate the challenge of supporting struggling learners without sacrificing the learning pace of the rest of their students.

And finally, you will find hope and real solutions to learning and attention challenges. Brain research in the last forty years and our experience over the last thirty-five have shown us that by identifying and developing the weak underlying learning/processing skills that provide the critical foundation for learning, and remediating the affected reading, writing, spelling, or math skills, most learning and attention challenges can be eliminated or changed.[1]

# TAKE THE STONE OUT OF THE SHOE

---

[1] The ground-breaking work of Glenn Doman and Carl Delacato with neurologically handicapped children, Patricia Lindamood with auditory discrimination and reading difficulties, and Michael Merzenich with neuroplasticity laid a foundation for understanding that underlying neurodevelopmental and processing skills support learning and can be effectively trained for permanent improvements in learning and thinking.

JILL STOWELL

Chapter One
# PARENTS, YOU'RE NOT ALONE

### I Hate Feeling Crazy!

My father-in-law loved instruction manuals. He would pour over the manual for any item he bought because he wanted to know exactly how it worked, all the things it could do, and what problems and solutions to expect.

But kids don't come with instruction manuals. So we all step into parenting a little blindly. It's a figure-it-out-as-you-go proposition from the start.

When we send our little five-year-olds off to kindergarten and imagine their school years ahead, we picture happy children who love school, have friends, learn easily, make good grades, and accomplish good things. If it doesn't turn out this way, if they begin to struggle or feel dumb, or fight and cry over homework, many parents feel lost and confused.

Now what? There's no instruction manual to tell them what to do.

Parents of smart but struggling students get conflicting messages from relatives, friends, and even teachers.

- He's a boy–he'll grow out of it.
- She just needs to try harder.

- If he was more motivated, he could do it.
- You worry too much!

Parents may begin to second-guess themselves. "Maybe I'm just paranoid. Maybe there's not really anything wrong; I'm just over-protective."

It's very hard to understand how smart kids can struggle in school, especially when those kids have other obvious talents. Our learning centers are full of smart, engaging students who have talents or abilities that simply don't seem to match their struggles in school. They may be very artistic, musically talented, mechanical and able to put anything together without looking at the directions, verbal and social, or great at sports.

If they can do those things, why do they struggle in school? How can a student excel in math but struggle in reading or vice versa? Parents shake their heads and think, "Am I just crazy?"

There are whole sets of underlying cognitive processing skills that support various types of thinking and learning. These are skills such as attention, memory, auditory and visual processing, motor control, processing speed, language comprehension, and reasoning. Weak or underdeveloped skills in one or more of these areas can cause smart children and adults to struggle.

Here's what I know about moms: they just know. They may not know what's causing the problem, but they know there's something. Recently, when I explained to a mom that her daughter's struggles were the result of mild dyslexia and weak auditory processing skills, she said, "That's exactly what I felt, but no one believed me. I *hate* feeling crazy!"

## Frightened for My Child

I was terrified when a zombie reached out from his hiding place and tried to grab me in the *Walking Dead* attraction at Universal Studios Hollywood. Once we left the exhibit, I was able to laugh it off and enjoy the fictitious close call.

It's fun to be scared when you know it's not real, but many parents spend years of sleepless nights feeling truly frightened for their children who have learning or attention challenges.

"What will happen when my child gets to high school?"

"Will my child be able to go to college or be an independent adult?"

"What damage is being done to my child's self-esteem when he tries so hard and still gets poor grades?"

"What if we try one more thing and it doesn't help?"

When children struggle in school, it's scary and confusing. Smart, talented kids can have mind-boggling struggles with reading or other academic skills. They seem to get something one day and forget it the next. Families spend hours and hours slaving over homework, often to see disappointing results.

Repeatedly, parents of struggling students share, not their desire for their child to be an A student, but their deep desire for their child to be able to become more independent.

This is exactly our goal at Stowell Learning Centers and what we know to be possible–to help children and adults with dyslexia and diagnosed or undiagnosed learning disabilities to become comfortable, independent learners.

## "I Want My Son to Love School Again"

I know a guy who was so unhappy in his job that he literally counted the hours until retirement for his entire last year of employment.

Struggling students often feel the same way about the end of the school year. They are counting the minutes until they are "free" and may already be dreading the start of school next year.

"I just want my son to love school again," said the mom of an eight-year-old boy. She went on to share that the summer before her son began kindergarten, he was so excited about starting school that he asked repeatedly, "Can I start today?"

That's how learning should feel! Like an adventure that we just can't wait to start!

But this boy, who started off so excited, now marks off each day on the calendar until he can get to a day with no school. He counted down the days to the end of his second-grade year and relief.

What saps the excitement out of learning? The same thing that saps the excitement out of anything–lack of success.

It is hard for parents, friends, relatives, and even some teachers to understand how an otherwise typical child can struggle in school. After all, everyone does it and it's not rocket science, right?

But learning requires tools. Just as a carpenter has sets of specific tools to create and build with, there are whole sets of underlying physical and mental tools that need to be in place in order to learn comfortably and effectively in school. When any of these underlying tools, or learning skills, are weak, it can cause students to have to work harder and longer than expected, and often with lesser results.

Children and teens spend a huge amount of time in school. Struggling students may find ways to compensate for their challenges, but after a while, those compensations take their toll in time, effort, energy, attention, and motivation.

A carpenter wouldn't dream of using a screwdriver to do a job that requires a hammer. So why would we expect a student to perform in school without the right tools?

I think the real answer to this question is that parents and most educators simply don't understand what the underlying learning skills are and, more importantly, that they can be developed.

We tend to accept that students have dyslexia, auditory or visual processing disorders, attention deficits, and learning disabilities and try to support them and give them workarounds, but you rarely hear people talking about actually correcting these challenges.

However, it is absolutely possible for a smart but struggling student to learn to love school again. The underlying skills that support learning can be developed. Like the carpenter, students *can* access the right tools for the job.

We have worked with thousands of children and adults over the past thirty-five years, developing the needed underlying learning skills and remediating the affected reading, writing, spelling, or math skills. We know it's possible, and the brain research over the past forty years proves that the brain can literally rewire itself.

I remember working with a boy with severe dyslexia and attention challenges when he was in the third grade. It was not a quick fix–we worked with him from third to sixth grade–but when he went on to junior high, no one could believe that he had struggled in school. By high school, he was able to play sports and independently handle honors classes.

As an elementary student, Kris hated school and tried to avoid it at all costs, but as his learning skills and reading changed, he found that he actually liked learning! When I ran into his mom a few years ago, she shared that Kris was an avid student and had just gone back to school for a second master's degree.

## Why Isn't the School Helping My Child?

Parents often feel discouraged with the schools. Families raw from spending hours and hours doing homework every night feel alone and frustrated that the schools aren't doing more.

As a former mainstream and special education teacher, I would like to shed a little light on the subject.

### *Doesn't qualify–no problem?*

Students with learning or attention challenges are often quite bright. In spite of their poor performance, their intelligence, coping strategies, and intense mental effort may cause them to score just high enough in a psycho-educational evaluation that they don't qualify as officially having a learning disability, making them exempt from special education help.

Parents are told that there is no problem and their child needs to try harder or put in more time. For parents crushed by their child's tears, frustration, and hours and hours of time spent on homework, this answer is just not acceptable. It makes them feel misunderstood and ignored.

Just because a child doesn't qualify for special education services at school doesn't mean there's not a problem. In fact, research backs up the fact that approximately 20–25 percent of students in school have some degree of struggle and do not qualify for special help.[2]

### "Special Ed isn't helping!"

I would venture to say that this is not true. But it *feels* true to parents who have to hear their defeated child say, day after day, "I'm so dumb."

Parents can see the bright child beneath the struggles and want the problem fixed. Many students, in spite of special education services, continue to struggle year after year. As a result, it often seems like the school is doing nothing.

The reality is that most of our students' teachers care deeply and are devastated to see the ongoing struggle so many of their students face. Teachers are required to teach subject areas and curriculum. There is a tremendous number of very specific skills and standards teachers are required to help their students meet. Even in special education, the job revolves around helping students acquire the required knowledge.

This is what schools do. It's their job. And thank goodness it is, as no one else is doing it.

But . . . academic success requires a strong foundation of underlying learning/processing skills. Weaknesses in any of those skills will stress both attention and learning.

If we want to correct a learning challenge, we have to determine what underlying skills are not supporting the learner well enough and develop those skills. Then the academic remediation will make sense and stick. Students with at least average intelligence can and should become comfortable independent learners.

At Stowell Learning Centers, we develop the critical underlying learning skills *and* remediate the basic academics–reading, writing, spelling, and math.

We do not take on the school's job of teaching higher academics. We don't have the time or training to do it. Schools do not take on our job of developing underlying skills. They don't generally have the time, knowledge, or funding to do it.

What schools do is try to support struggling learners as they navigate academic subjects. They don't eliminate the problem. Most don't even realize that the problem can be eliminated. That's frustrating, as kids spend a tremendous number of hours in school.

But parents, look at teachers as your allies. Help them understand and empathize with your child. A supportive teacher can bolster a child's self-esteem and confidence and help him manage his academics better than he would without the support.

Then look for outside help to get those underlying skills identified and improved. A combination of school support and outside development of skills will be your child's best bet.

## Why Does the School Say He's Fine When He's Failing Two Classes and Barely Passing the Rest?

Good question!

Is it because as a teenager, he looks mature and like he should have the skills to be doing better?

Is it because he's now so discouraged that he acts like he doesn't care?

Is it because his work doesn't reflect his intelligence, making it look like the issue is just a lack of effort?

A therapist in our Learning Center Network brought a student to my attention. He's not one of our students, but he could be, because he faced a similar incongruity to many of our students: poor grades, poor test scores, but the parent was told the student was doing fine.

This particular high school student–let's call him Zach –was found to be dyslexic and have both auditory processing and comprehension delays based on my colleague's testing.

I think the struggles of students like Zach get missed or overlooked for a variety of reasons:

1. Students with dyslexia or other learning disabilities often look and act just like their peers, so the poor performance is mistaken for what might be lack of effort or motivation in a typical student.

2. Parents help their struggling students so much with homework that the poor grades are a reflection of low test scores, leaving the perception that the student is not studying hard enough.

3. These students are masters at hiding or compensating for their struggles, so it may look like they're fine, but they're not.

4. It is a common belief that dyslexia and learning disabilities are a permanent condition, so barely passing with a C or having to retake a few classes in the summer becomes acceptable.

When students struggle in school, we need to ask the question, "What is keeping this otherwise bright, capable student from reading, learning, or performing as well as he should?"

To find the answer, we have to identify what underlying learning/processing skills are weak or not supporting the student well enough.

Then we need to sweep away the old myth that says that learning and attention challenges cannot be changed–that the person must just accept and learn to live with them.

Forty years of brain research and our experience with thousands of children and adults with learning and attention challenges has shown us that by identifying and developing the weak underlying learning/processing skills that provide the critical foundation for learning, most learning and attention challenges can be dramatically improved or completely corrected.

If you are being told that your child is doing fine but you see signs that tell you he is struggling, you are probably right. And the way to change that is by getting to the real root of the problem.

### Did I Waste Time and Money on Therapy?

Several years ago, we had a student whose challenges with speech articulation were so significant that his mom explained on our first meeting that there were certain sounds that he could not physically say.

Grayson was eleven and had had private speech therapy as well as speech services at school for most of his life. After three weeks of sessions at Stowell Learning Center, Grayson was able to say every sound both in isolation and in connected speech. His speech therapist at school, who did not know he was attending the Learning Center, said at his IEP meeting, "Have you noticed how much clearer Grayson's speech has gotten in the last three weeks?"

As I walked through the waiting room in one of our centers, a mom shared with me that after five years of speech therapy at school, her son no longer qualified for services. She was thrilled. Speech, she said, had not been making a difference for some time, but after three months at the Learning Center, he had made so much progress that he no longer needed the extra help with speech at school.

It made my day to see this mom so happy and to hear how life at home was changing for all of them as a result of their work at the Learning Center. Do we get to take all the credit? No, not really. It takes the patience and persistence of parents, and I have no doubt that all of the previous support provided to our students at school and through other therapies play a part.

Here's why we can see changes that don't seem to occur with other interventions. Learning, including speaking, paying attention, organization, reading, spelling, math, and writing, is built upon a foundation of underlying processing skills. These are skills such as auditory and visual processing, attention, body awareness and control, memory, and reasoning. These are not typically taught, but rather are assumed to be in place when children go to school. When any of these underlying skills are weak, it can cause students to struggle more than would be expected.

In the case of our students with speech challenges, the weak area was auditory processing. This is not a person's hearing, but rather the way the brain perceives and thinks about the information that comes in through the ears. Auditory processing has a dramatic impact on speech, communication, reading, comprehension, social skills, and learning in general.

Weak auditory processing may cause a person to get incomplete, inaccurate, confusing, or delayed information when listening–kind of like a bad cell phone connection. Dr. Alfred Tomatis, a pioneer in sound therapy research, said that we cannot reproduce what we cannot hear. For our students with trouble clearly enunciating sounds and pronouncing words, improving auditory processing allows them to hear or process the sounds and words more accurately, which then makes it possible for them to say them more accurately and clearly as well.

### Were previous therapies a waste?

No, most likely not. But if those therapies did not work as well as hoped or expected, there were almost certainly underlying skills that were not providing the needed foundation for what was being taught. Developing the needed processing/learning skills allows the previously taught skills, as well as any current remediation, to make more sense and stick.

### "I Don't Want My Son Accommodated!"

A frustrated mom of a seven-year-old with reading challenges said, emphatically, "I don't want my son accommodated!"

This is not a stubborn parent or a parent in denial. Of course she wants supports in place at school to help her son *feel* more successful. But fewer spelling words or taking tests orally, while valuable at the moment, are not going to help her son *be* successful.

# TAKE THE STONE OUT OF THE SHOE

It is natural and good to try to help people out when they struggle, so if the school is offering help to your child, you should take it. We want adults paying attention to our kids. But it's important to understand that accommodations are not a permanent solution. They are temporary support.

Accommodating a learning problem is like teaching someone to ride a bike when the bike has a flat tire. It's possible to do it, but it will always take extra energy, time, and effort, and it will never be as easy and enjoyable as it should be. And what happens when the supportive hand is no longer there? We say, "Why not just fix the tire?"

Brain research tells us that the brain has plasticity, or the ability to change with training. Through intensive training that stretches an individual's thinking, chemical and physical changes can occur in the brain. Because we know this kind of neuro-rehabilitation is possible, we also know that with the right tools and strategies, new, more efficient neuropathways can be developed to permanently improve students' overall processing and performance. Accommodations have their place, but they should not become a lifestyle!

---

[2] Patricia Lindamood's research on phonological awareness indicated that 30 percent of students have some degree of difficulty with this key auditory processing skill that impacts reading and spelling. In 2019–2020, the NCES (National Center for Education) reported that approximately 5 percent of public school students were receiving special education services for learning disabilities.

Chapter Two
# I WISH MY PARENTS AND TEACHERS UNDERSTOOD HOW I FEEL

### Mom, Am I Dumb?

I met a delightful mom who was trying to understand and get help for her equally delightful eight-year-old boy. She shared that he came home from school asking, "Mom, am I dumb?"

I've heard this scenario so many times over the years. Why would a smart child or teen or adult think they're dumb?

When you're smart but struggling, you look around the classroom, and you can easily see that your peers are finishing assignments quicker or getting better grades. You're very aware of the tremendous amount of time it takes you to do your homework, while others in the neighborhood are already done and out playing. You know how hard you studied for the test, but you got an embarrassing grade anyway.

So, you figure, you must not be all that smart.

I met a man at a seminar once who said that he couldn't read until he was twelve. He hated going to school because he felt so dumb. But the truth was, he was brilliant, and by the time he was twenty-one, he had figured out strategies for playing the stock market that made him a millionaire.

In order to learn easily, we need to be able to pay attention, remember, and receive clear and accurate information through our visual, auditory, and motor systems. When any of these underlying thinking/processing skills are weak, it can cause learning to be a struggle.

Struggling learners and their families are told to cope with the learning challenge and find ways to get around it. Most parents that we speak to refuse to believe that coping is the answer. And they are right!

### I'm Not a Reading Person

I had the pleasure of testing two very bright and very different dyslexic students in the same week. One was nine. We'll call him Chris.

Chris had tremendous confusion with letters. He not only reversed *b* and *d*, but most other similar-looking letters, such as *h* and *n*; *i* and *l*; and *t*, *f*, and *j*. He read by guessing at words based on the first and last letter in the word.

When I asked him if it was difficult to look at the words on the page, he said, "I'm not a reading person."

He went on to say that if he looked at words for too long, they got fuzzy and he'd close his eyes to make the fuzziness disappear. Matter-of-factly, he said, "But I can handle it most of the time."

Chris was definitely not a reading person–at least not at that time. As a fourth grader, he could not read, but he certainly made a valiant attempt at it.

Isn't it amazing what our kids do to survive–to try to do what's expected!

The other young man, Jack, was sixteen. He also had dyslexia, but he had managed to maintain fairly acceptable performance in regular high school classes. He seemed to do well on homework but failed most tests. So the question being asked by Jack's parents, teachers, and even himself was, "Are the low test scores the result of poor motivation to study, lack of focus, anxiety, or poor attention?"

The teenage years come with some attitude. And if you continually try hard and get a disappointing result, your attitude may indicate that you don't really care, but here's what I saw with Jack:

Jack was putting out an exceptional amount of mental energy to manage at school. He was bright enough and quietly determined enough that the challenges he faced were subtle to others looking on, but for him, the cost was performance anxiety and deteriorating self-esteem.

Working with Jack and Chris reminded me, again, how hard students with dyslexia and other learning challenges work each and every hour in school. Because they often can't compete with their peers, even with excessive time, effort, and energy, it may look like they aren't trying their best. Coping with a learning or attention challenge day in and day out is exhausting. In virtually every case, beneath the surface of poor grades, homework battles, and inconsistent performance is a student who is putting out far more mental energy and effort than the top students in the class.

Learning to read, spell, and write easily and automatically depends upon a solid set of underlying learning/processing skills. The auditory system in the brain has to be able to process the number, order, and identity of sounds in words (phonemic awareness). The visual system has to be able to see and discriminate each letter and word on the page clearly and in the correct order. The brain has to be able to notice and pay attention to small, common sight words such as *the*, *of*, and *if* that don't always follow the phonetic rules and don't connect easily with a concept or mental image. The language part of the brain has to be able to understand, sequence, and associate the meaning of the words and sentences.

Without these critical auditory, visual, and language processing skills, reading just doesn't work. If any one of these areas is weak, learners will struggle more than they should with reading and/or spelling or writing.

## I Can't Read a Thing, but My Teacher Thinks I'm a Reader! –*Dyslexic Second Grader*

How is it possible for a dyslexic non-reader to fool her parents and teacher to the point that they honestly believe she can read?

Dyslexic learners are generally quite bright and often have very good comprehension. If they also have good language and memory skills, they may be able to memorize the stories–especially in first or second grade.

I have found our dyslexic students, both children and adults, to be remarkable. They are very perceptive and creative. They know what a reader should look like and can mimic the behavior even though they struggle to read and write. If they can recognize enough of the words, they can make fairly good guesses about the context and use their deductive reasoning to answer questions.

# TAKE THE STONE OUT OF THE SHOE

If they can't read enough of the words, I've seen many dyslexic students simply make up their own story with such good inflection that they sound like they really are reading.

Some dyslexic students get very disoriented when looking at the words on the page. The words may seem to move around, disappear, or change places. Some students have said that if they look at the words too long, the sentences turn into lines across the page. To counteract this, students may read extremely fast, filling in whatever seems to make sense to them. Their reading is inaccurate, but it's so fast that the listener may not be sure what was said and not pick it up.

Fluent, easy reading requires an internal understanding of the sounds in words and the ability to decode automatically. Dyslexic students have varying degrees of challenge with processing the sounds and sounding out words. When this is a key issue for them, they often mumble or slur through words they don't know. Instead of recognizing the reading problem, others may think the student is shy or just speaks softly.

I have seen dyslexic students successfully hide their extremely weak reading behind being the class clown, the sports star, the actor, the social butterfly, or the sweet just-under-the-radar helper. They may use their intelligence to deduce answers when they really haven't been able to read most of the text.

I am in awe of the ingenuity of our dyslexic students as they find ways to hide their challenges and navigate the world of print without really being able to read at the level needed. One student we tested got all the way into medical school before his compensations for a dyslexic thinking style and his sixth-grade reading level caught up with him.

Being able to compensate is a survival mechanism that helps students manage socially and in school, but the ramifications can be many in the long run:

- Stress and anxiety
- Poor performance misunderstood by parents and teachers
- Feeling stupid because they have to work so much harder and longer than others and do poorly anyway
- Not getting the help they need because it seems like they can do it

Compensations only last for so long, and at some point, the student simply can't keep up with the demands of the grade level.

The good news is that most dyslexic challenges can be corrected. The underlying auditory and visual memory and processing skills that support being able to read and spell can be identified and retrained so students with dyslexia and other reading challenges can learn to read! This takes specialized and intensive cognitive training and reading/spelling remediation, but it is absolutely possible.

Dyslexic learners can keep their talents and creative thinking style *and* become proficient, independent readers, and it is possible at any age.

### This Is So Boring!

"I hate History. It's boring."

"I don't want to do this homework. It's so borrrring!" (Said in a whiney voice.)

# TAKE THE STONE OUT OF THE SHOE

If you're the parent of a school-age student, you've probably heard this before. If you're the parent of a child who struggles in school, you have probably heard this, or something similar, more times than you can count.

The definition of boring is "not interesting; tedious." And there certainly are assignments that are just plain boring.

But for many students with learning challenges, "boring" translates as, "I think this is too hard and I may not be able to do it," or, "This makes me feel stupid and I don't want to have to deal with it."

When kids are struggling, it's particularly important to listen between the lines.

In the book, *The Orphan Train*, a teenage foster child, when asked why she hasn't tried to find out what's happening with her biological mom, says, "I don't care, that's why." But the truth was, she did care. She cared desperately, but she was so afraid of the answer that it was easier to put on a defiant face and tell herself and the world that she didn't care.

At the Stowell Learning Center, when a student says something is boring or digs in about trying a particular task or activity, our job is to determine what is making that task something to be avoided. What about it is hard or overwhelming? How can we break it down so the student can feel success? What underlying skills does the student need to build so the task is not just manageable, but also something the student can do efficiently and comfortably?

What's really amazing is that once a student really understands something or feels competent with a task, it's suddenly no longer "boring" but "fun."

Reading will be excessively boring if you have to sound out every letter and the words still don't make sense when you put them together, or if the information you read just goes in one ear and out the other with no comprehension. Where's the fun in that?

But once your brain can process the sounds, connect them to the letters, and blend them together easily and automatically, reading can become a pleasure instead of a chore.

When the reader who doesn't remember or comprehend learns to create a mental movie while reading, a whole new exciting world opens up.

## Learning Differences Don't Really Make Me Different!

In Southern California, we are the very definition of a melting pot. We have people of every color, culture, and religion from every part of the world. I love that! I think it makes us interesting.

One of the things I've noticed, working with thousands of families who are dealing with learning and attention challenges, is that no matter what differences are evident on the surface, parents are parents. If their child is suffering, so are they. They shed tears over their kids, they search for answers, and they willingly sacrifice to help.

Struggling in school makes smart students feel like they're different. The truth is dyslexia, learning disabilities, and attention challenges do make them different.

But in the most fundamental ways, they are not different at all. Like everyone else, students with learning and attention challenges have good innate intelligence and their own set of talents or abilities. They want to do well, have friends, and be accepted. They thrive with praise and success and wilt under repeated failure–just like everyone else.

Learning disabilities have been called "Invisible Disabilities" because in so many cases, you would never suspect that these students struggle in school. We have centers full of bright, motivated students who struggle, sometimes quite terribly, with reading, math, writing, speaking, or getting their work done. But outside the academic arena, they are athletes, musicians, artists, actors, and Lego masters. They are silly, friendly, motivated, and kind.

So learning differences don't really make them that different–they're just kids, after all–but learning differences do get in the way of students working as comfortably and independently as they should.

Thankfully, this can change. It's not a quick-and-easy fix, but it's not a forever process either. With intensity and consistency and an emphasis on improving the weak underlying thinking/learning skills that are causing the problem, children, teens, and adults can eliminate or dramatically change their learning or attention challenges.

### What if "Try Harder" Isn't the Answer?

Ashley was a bright, popular, engaging eleventh grader who was failing history and barely scraping by in her other classes. Her parents and teachers were extremely frustrated with her underachievement and were adamant that if she would just try harder, she would get better grades. Her parents were fearful for her future, as her apparent lack of effort was going to impact her chances of getting into college.

When we tested Ashley, we found that she could read, write, spell, and do math, but her auditory processing speed, working memory, and reasoning skills were weak and inconsistent. As a result, she didn't always hear the instructions or get all the lecture information. She rarely finished her tests or homework, and when she did, her grades were discouragingly low.

Ashley said she tried very hard for her first two years in high school, but it didn't seem to make a difference. By eleventh grade, she had pretty much given up and put her energy into being social, an arena where she could excel.

Ashley did a program with us to build her processing skills. Before her twelve-week program was completed, her attitude about school, as well as her grades, completely turned around. By the end of the semester, this former hater of history had the highest grade in the class.

Many parents share with me that their kids are so smart and try so hard, but in spite of all that effort, they fail tests or get low grades anyway. They and their children are incredibly discouraged.

If trying harder gets you results, then it's worth the effort, but for many students with learning and attention challenges, trying harder just ends in disappointment. All the motivation and effort in the world won't get you the results you want if you don't have the skills to do the job.

There is a whole continuum of underlying skills that support easy, efficient learning. These are skills such as memory, attention, and auditory and visual processing that are not really taught anywhere but are assumed to be in place when kids go to school. If any of the critical underlying skills, or mental tools, are weak, it will likely impact their learning.

It's not fair and it's frustrating, but thankfully, these underlying skills can be improved–often dramatically or completely. It's not a quick-and-easy fix, but strengthening weak underlying processing/learning skills for a student with learning or attention challenges is a turning point in their life.

JILL STOWELL

Chapter Three
# UNDERSTANDING THE PROBLEM BENEATH THE PROBLEM

## The Skills Behind School Success: The Learning Skills Continuum

The Learning Skills Continuum is a hierarchy of skills that follows natural human development beginning with movement and self-awareness; increasing to include awareness, understanding, and interaction with the world around us; and finally, higher-level learning and self-management skills.

If you think about learning like a ladder or a continuum, academics and school subjects are at the very top. Many other skills must be in place in order to provide the supports needed to learn and function well with those academic and school skills at the top. Imagine that you are doing a job at the top of a ladder but some of the rungs below are wobbly or unstable. Where will your attention be focused? Most likely, not fully on the job. Your brain will be much more concerned with not falling off of the ladder.

In the same way, compensating for weak underlying skills will divert attention and energy from the learning task. When the underlying learning skills, or skills lower on the continuum are weak, they may keep children and adults from learning and functioning as well and as independently as they should.

We all understand the top levels of the continuum because these are school skills: reading, spelling, writing, math, and other content areas. But what are the underlying skills that are needed to support comfortable, independent learning in the academic areas? From bottom up on the continuum, they are as follows:

### *Core Learning Skills*

These are foundational movement, visual, and auditory skills that help children develop a sense of self, internal organization, and body and attention awareness and control. Core learning skills start developing at birth and are the foundation for all learning. These are our body control skills that allow us to move through space easily, to sit in a chair, hold a pencil, and move our eyes across the page for reading. These skills should be so automatic that we don't have to think about them. If we have to consciously think about sitting still and being in control of our body, attention will get funneled away from learning.

### *Processing Skills*

These are skills such as attention, memory, auditory and visual processing (how we think about and understand things that we hear or see), processing speed, language comprehension, and phonological awareness (the thinking process critical to reading that supports learning and using phonics).

### *Executive Function*

This is our personal manager that guides and directs our attention and behavior. It helps us reason, problem solve, organize, and make and evaluate our decisions.

TAKE THE STONE OUT OF THE SHOE

Here is a diagram of the Learning Skills Continuum, followed by a list of some of the skills in each area:

# The **Learning Skills** Continuum

Having a learning challenge is like doing a job at the top of a ladder when some of rungs underneath are unstable. This diverts attention and causes everything to be harder and take longer. By strengthening underlying skills (the rungs), attention, confidence, and success at the top of the ladder improve!

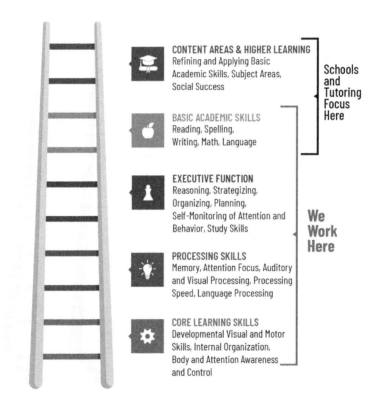

**CONTENT AREAS & HIGHER LEARNING**
Refining and Applying Basic Academic Skills, Subject Areas, Social Success

**BASIC ACADEMIC SKILLS**
Reading, Spelling, Writing, Math, Language

} Schools and Tutoring Focus Here

**EXECUTIVE FUNCTION**
Reasoning, Strategizing, Organizing, Planning, Self-Monitoring of Attention and Behavior, Study Skills

**PROCESSING SKILLS**
Memory, Attention Focus, Auditory and Visual Processing, Processing Speed, Language Processing

**CORE LEARNING SKILLS**
Developmental Visual and Motor Skills, Internal Organization, Body and Attention Awareness and Control

} We Work Here

www.StowellCenter.com

© Green Dot Press 2010
Developed By Jill Stowell, MS | Author | Learning Disability Specialist | Dyslexia Remediation Specialist

Motor, Visual, Auditory, Language, Attention, Memory, and Executive Function Systems develop and are used with increasing sophistication as one moves up the continuum. Higher level success is dependent upon a solid lower level foundation.

© Green Dot Press 2010
Developed By Jill Stowell, MS | Author | Learning Disability Specialist | Dyslexia Remediation Specialist

# TAKE THE STONE OUT OF THE SHOE

## The Learning Skills Continuum Approach to Permanently Changing Learning and Attention Challenges

The Learning Skills Continuum provides an understanding of the skills needed to learn and function optimally and becomes a guide for evaluating and developing both the academic skills and the numerous underlying skills that support effective learning.

The Continuum Approach applies brain science to learning. Brain research on neuroplasticity has proven that through targeted and intensive training, the brain can literally change and grow. New and permanent neuropathways or connections can be made that will allow individuals to learn new skills and process information more effectively.

Students with learning and attention challenges come to us with their own unique set of strengths and weaknesses in both their underlying skills and academics. Their challenges may be in just one area, but more often are a compilation of a number of skills in different areas. Working with the whole continuum of skills allows us to create a comprehensive plan for each individual student and makes it possible for a wide number of issues to be addressed in one place instead of families having to find and participate in many different therapies.

## Does Your Child Have the Right Tools for the Job?

A homeschool mom shared that her teenage son was bright and willing but getting increasingly frustrated and depressed over his struggles with schoolwork.

She said, "I feel like I'm asking him to dig a hole, but I don't know what kind of shovel to give him." My husband is fond of saying, "If the only tool you have is a hammer, everything looks like a nail." But the bottom line is that even though a hammer may be an excellent tool, it isn't the right tool to do all jobs.

Struggling learners tend to have a pattern of real strengths and weaknesses in their underlying processing/learning skills, causing them to have to over-rely on their strengths. For example:

- A student with a weak ability to think about the sounds in words (phonological awareness) may be dependent upon his memorized vocabulary for reading. Because he can't sound out unfamiliar words, his reading may be inaccurate or slow because he has to reread over and over in order to figure out the words.
- A student with good verbal skills but a weak ability to get information from head to paper may chat with neighbors instead of doing his work, or put excessive energy into talking his way out of things.
- A student with weak comprehension skills may rely on rote memory to write down everything the teacher says, or memorize her study guide exactly, resulting in very dense and unhelpful notes and poor test scores. Questions phrased differently than the study guide will seem like completely different information.

Having the right tools always makes the job easier. The Learning Skills Continuum provides a tool for understanding and exploring each student's set of learning tools.

## What Does It Really Mean When the School Says Your Struggling Student Doesn't Have a Learning Disability?

I have spoken with many parents who are confused and distraught because they see their child struggling with anxiety and frustration over schoolwork every day, yet the school testing did not show a learning disability.

Does that mean that the parent is crazy? Overprotective?

Does it mean that the student really could do the work if he cared enough?

Does it mean that the school is lying so they don't have to pay for special education services?

**No, no, and no.**

Patricia Lindamood's research tells us that about 30 percent of the population has some degree of difficulty with a critical underlying auditory processing skill needed for reading and spelling. That means that nearly one in three students in every classroom will have some difficulty with reading or spelling, and that's related to just one of the many, many underlying learning skills that need to be in place to learn comfortably and efficiently.

Current statistics on dyslexia indicate that approximately one in five students, or 15–20 percent of the population, has a language-based learning disability, of which dyslexia is the most common.

When testing is done at school, it is to see if students fall within specific parameters that would qualify them to use public funds for special education services. The discrepancy between the student's intellectual potential and academic achievement has to be very, very large. Only about 5–9 percent of students qualify as having a learning disability.

That means that at least 20–25 percent of struggling students don't actually qualify as having a learning disability in spite of the challenges their parents and teachers see.

At Stowell Learning Center, we do what is called a Functional Academic and Learning Skills Assessment. Our goal is not to diagnose or qualify students, but rather to determine the root cause of the struggles with learning or attention parents are reporting to us.

Brain research over the last four decades has shown that with intensive and targeted brain training, the brain can literally rewire itself. This is very encouraging. It means that whether or not your child qualifies as having a learning disability, the challenge can be addressed and permanently changed by identifying and developing the weak underlying processing/learning skills that are at the root of the problem.

Parents: The school isn't lying to you if they say your child doesn't qualify as having a learning disability. But you are not wrong about what you see either. Struggles with learning and attention don't have to have a formal diagnosis to wreak havoc with your child's school performance and self-esteem.

## 5 Reasons Why Your Child's Attention Problem Might NOT be ADHD

"Your child just can't seem to pay attention in class. It could be ADHD."

# TAKE THE STONE OUT OF THE SHOE

Yes. It *could* be ADHD, but did you know that there are *many* other reasons why kids struggle to pay attention in class and when doing homework? At Stowell Learning Centers, the vast majority of our students have attention challenges, but only a very small minority actually have ADHD.

**Jeremy** wiggles constantly in his chair. It keeps him from getting his work done and is very distracting to the students sitting near him.

**Manny** talks to his neighbors all the time instead of doing his work. He's always interested in what everyone else is doing, but he can't seem to pay attention to his own work.

**Sara** tries really hard to be good. She sits up tall and looks right at the teacher. But pretty soon, she's fiddling with things on her desk or staring straight through the teacher. When it's time to start working, Sara always has to ask, "What were we supposed to do?"

**Rachel** never knows what she's supposed to do for homework. She uses her planner, but what she's written is incomplete and doesn't make a lot of sense. If she does do her homework, she usually can't find it when it's time to turn it in.

**Jessica** is getting Ds and Fs in high school. She can read, write, spell, and do math, but she doesn't pay attention in class, does poorly on tests, and doesn't get her work done.

### What do these students have in common?

Each of these students has trouble paying attention in class, yet not one of them has attention deficit disorder.

Poor attention in class may be a symptom, not the real problem. If a child has problems with any of the underlying learning skills, his attention system will also be stressed. While attention may *become* a problem in school or with homework, it may not actually *be* the real problem.

**Jeremy**, our wiggly, distracting student can't sit still in his chair because of a retained primitive reflex called the *spinal Galant*.

Primitive reflexes are involuntary movements that are present in infants to help with the birthing process and adaptation as a newborn. If these reflexes don't disappear within about the first year of life, they may continue to fire and cause neurological interference to efficient development and easy learning.

Jeremy's retained spinal Galant reflex causes him to wiggle in his chair when he doesn't mean to. When he tries hard to sit still, it takes all of his attention, so he can't really think about what the teacher is saying or what he's supposed to be doing on his assignments.

**Manny** is dyslexic. He's very smart and very clever. He has memorized some words, but he can't sound out new words, and sometimes when he looks at the page, it seems like the words and letters are moving around. At nine years old, he's already figured out that getting in trouble for entertaining his neighbors is better than anyone knowing he can't read.

**Sara** has an auditory processing problem. She tries hard to listen, but what she hears is spotty and inconsistent, like a bad cell phone connection. She tries to fill in the gaps, but pretty soon, it just doesn't make sense, and she can't keep her attention on it anymore.

**Rachel** has poor visual memory skills. When she tries to copy down assignments, she has to look back and forth so many times between the board and her planner that she often loses her place and misses part of the information. It takes her longer than the other students, so she often doesn't finish because it's embarrassing to have to stay after class to copy the assignment.

When Rachel does her homework, she sticks it in her backpack. The problem is, she can't hold a picture in her mind of exactly where it is, so when it's time to turn it in the next day, she can't remember where she put it. Well-meaning teachers and family have suggested that maybe medication would help her pay better attention. They don't realize that Rachel *is* paying attention, but her visual memory is not supporting her well enough to remember the information.

**Jessica** has weak processing and executive function skills. She's pretty sure her parents and teacher are right when they say she's lazy and unmotivated because she just can't seem to pay attention and get her work done.

Weak underlying processing and executive function skills can keep capable students from being able to pull it all together to perform as expected. They struggle to keep up and have inconsistent homework grades and test scores.

## Addressing the root cause of the poor attention symptoms can eliminate the problem

All five of these students were able to solve their attention and learning challenges by developing their lagging underlying learning skills.

**Jeremy** went through Core Learning Skills Training to integrate his retained reflexes and improve his body awareness and control. He no longer stands out in class.

**Manny** went through a specialized auditory stimulation and reading program to develop his phonological awareness and ability to look at the words on the page without getting disoriented.

He can now understand how the sounds in words work and has learned to read and spell. He's putting his strong verbal abilities and humor to use in the school play.

**Sara** went through a program of Auditory Stimulation and Training to increase her auditory processing skills. She is able to listen to her teacher and her friends now without getting exhausted and missing information. She no longer feels lost and anxious and is able to be the good student she always tried to be.

**Rachel** received training in various visual processing, visual memory, and organization skills.

She can now copy from the board and use her planner accurately most of the time. She is more organized and can remember where her homework is in her backpack.

**Jessica** did an intensive processing skills program called PACE.[3] With a stronger foundation of processing/learning skills, she brought her grades up to As and Bs.

### Don't ignore attention problems in school

Problems paying attention in class can be a sign to parents that their child is struggling in school. This should not be ignored. But parents and teachers should be aware that whenever an area of underlying processing or learning skills is inefficient, extra energy will be needed to perform. This stresses the person's attention. It is important to look very carefully to determine if the attention challenges seen in class are the cause of the learning problem or the symptom.

## Dyslexia or ADHD?

Two young boys came to us with very similar learning strengths and challenges. In testing, they both had good attention, but one became squirmy in his chair whenever he had to read.

The squirmy little guy had been diagnosed with ADD (attention deficit disorder without hyperactivity). He was never a problem in class but was reported to spend time staring off into space when he was supposed to be reading or doing seatwork.

Medication had been prescribed, but his parents opted not to use it, as they weren't convinced that ADD was the real problem.

Most likely, these parents were right on target. Both of the boys showed strong dyslexic symptoms and had a family history of dyslexia and reading challenges. Their symptoms included the following:

- Good intelligence
- Good comprehension
- Strong ability to visualize pictures and real things (versus letters and words)
- Creative thinking
- Weak ability to retain an accurate image of words (sight words for reading and spelling)

- Weak phonological awareness (ability to think about the sounds and sound groupings in words)
- Extremely poor decoding skills (sounding out words)
- Visual disorientation when looking at the page. (One boy said the letters looked 3D. One said the letters got bigger and smaller.)

Like many dyslexic students, these boys were misunderstood at school. One was so verbal and charming that only his parents knew how much he was struggling and how much effort and time it took for him to read and write. At school, he was perceived as a bright verbal child who didn't always put in his best effort on schoolwork.

The second boy was just young enough and his skills were just strong enough that no one (except his parents) believed that there was a reading problem. When he looked at the page, the letters and words were hard to look at, and the sounds didn't really make sense. He used his powers of deduction from pictures, his own knowledge, and what he had memorized from group reading to basically figure out what the page might say and answer the questions. But often, his mind drifted away from this taxing process, so he'd been pegged as ADD. And, after all, what he could create in his mind was far more entertaining than a jumble of words and letters that didn't really make sense.

Using the Learning Skills Continuum as a guide in evaluation helps identify the real root of students' struggles in school. In the case of our two boys, the weak underlying skills at the root of the struggles specifically related to the processing of sounds in words and neuro-timing (which can trigger typical dyslexic symptoms and disorientation on the page).

Having a family history of dyslexia, the parents of the two boys had always heard that dyslexia could not be corrected–that you just have to cope with it. This is simply not true. ADD meds will not solve dyslexic challenges, but retraining the auditory and visual systems to process the sounds and letters on the page accurately gets the brain ready to learn, retain, and comfortably use reading and spelling skills.

Exploring the full range of underlying skills when evaluating struggling students is critical to identifying, addressing, and permanently correcting the actual cause of the problem.

---

[3] PACE is a proprietary processing skills program developed by LearningRx. PACE is provided by trained and certified providers.

Chapter Four
# WHAT DO CHALLENGES WITH CORE LEARNING SKILLS LOOK LIKE?

### Challenges at the Core Learning Skills Level

Core Learning Skills are basic movement, visual, and auditory skills that help children develop a sense of self, internal organization, and body and attention awareness and control. Challenges in this area might show up as follows:

- Poor posture
- Being awkward or uncoordinated
- Fatigue and low stamina
- Anxiety
- Lying on desk
- Confusion with directions, spatial orientation, letter reversals
- Hard time getting started or following through
- Lack of organization – always losing or forgetting things
- Poor handwriting
- Inability to sit still
- Trouble getting self going

- Meltdowns; short fuse
- Poor attention
- Rigidity both physically and mentally–great difficulty with change
- Disconnectedness, being spacey, seeming to "float" through life

**Why Is Change So Hard?**

Once when I was traveling in Europe, I heard some American tourists grumbling that things just weren't the same in Europe as they are at home! "Of course not," I thought. "Isn't that why we travel to other countries, to experience something different?"

Most of us do like routine and predictability in our lives most of the time, but a little change now and then keeps life interesting–variety is the spice of life, and all that.

But some children (and some adults) are extremely inflexible. They are completely disrupted by change. Going out for tacos on Friday night instead of pizza may throw some children into a complete tailspin.

Not just learning, but social skills and overall functioning as well, are supported by the numerous underlying learning/processing skills on the Learning Skills Continuum. The more solid these foundational skills are, the more flexible we can be. When there are weak areas in the underlying foundation, people can become rigid and stuck because it's too scary or may not feel safe to try something different:

- If I can't process what you say, I have to stick with topics I know.

- If my body is not in control, I have to stay rigid so I don't bump someone or knock something over and get into trouble.
- If I can't visually process my environment well or fast enough, I have to dig in so I don't have to feel insecure with new places or things.
- If I do things the way I always do, then I can predict the result. If I have to do something in a different way, I don't know what will happen.

These rigid behaviors can look like stubbornness, defiance, or obsessiveness–and they are–but the behaviors are often rooted in weak underlying learning/processing skills.

At the most basic level of Core Learning Skills, much of the communication flowing between the brain and body via our nervous system happens as a result of reflexes. Reflexes that are active when not needed or not active when needed create glitches in that communication.

Unintegrated reflexes, or reflexes that are not working properly, cause stress to our whole system and push us into fight-or-flight mode. Spending too much time in fight or flight when we don't actually need to be fighting or running for survival, can lead to rigid, anxious behavior and fear of change.

At a little higher level in the brain, auditory and visual processing, memory, or processing speed challenges can cause students to feel lost and insecure. Once again, sticking with what they know and resisting change is often the route these students take in order to maintain control.

Thankfully, we know now from decades of clinical evidence and research that reflexes can be integrated and the brain can be retrained or rewired to process information more easily.

Once the lagging underlying skills are identified and developed, the person can experience a greater sense of security and confidence. Strong underlying learning/processing skills contribute to mental flexibility and easier learning.

Making and keeping friends also becomes easier and more likely, as kids are able to be more flexible, try a different way, and see other points of view.

## Why Does My Child Act This Way?
*How retained reflexes impact behavior and learning*

A big snowstorm on the East Coast caused over two thousand airline flights to be canceled. I assume people got to their destinations eventually, but I also imagine that it caused a great deal of anxiety and disruption to people's lives.

Just as air travel is dependent upon an organized system of flight patterns, our nervous system is organized around a system of reflexes. Primitive reflexes support survival and development in infants, to be replaced with higher-level reflexes as the brain and muscles mature. Reflexes need to be working properly in order for us to move through life with ease and flow.

When reflexes are not integrated, or working properly, they are like cancelled flights and closed airports, causing disruption, disorganization, and distress to the person's functioning, attention, learning, and family.

# TAKE THE STONE OUT OF THE SHOE

Properly working reflexes are critical to optimal functioning. Retained or unintegrated reflexes are often at the root of the behavior that causes parents to worry and wonder, "Why does my child act this way?"

Did you know:

- Bedwetting beyond the age of five and sleep problems may be related to a retained spinal Perez reflex?
- A child who hates to wear shoes may have a retained Babinski reflex.
- The child who continually drops or knocks things over when he turns his head may have a retained ATNR (asymmetrical tonic neck reflex)?
- A child who appears aggressive, defiant, or prone to temper tantrums may have a retained fear paralysis reflex?
- An infant with problems nursing may have an inactive grasping reflex?
- A child who craves sweets and tends to snack rather than eat whole meals may have a retained Moro reflex?
- A student with memory and reading problems may have a retained STNR (symmetrical tonic neck reflex)?
- A student who speaks well but can't get her thoughts on paper may have a retained ATNR?
- A student with poor organizational skills may have an unintegrated Landau reflex?

The list goes on and on. To me, it is fascinating to see how everything is connected. Frustrating or difficult behaviors and challenges with learning are related to something. They are not about not caring, being unmotivated, bad parenting, or being "bad kids." They are related to reflexes and underlying skills that are not supporting the person well enough.

The encouraging thing is that these reflexes can be integrated and weak underlying skills can be developed. When the pathways are open, the brain is available and ready to pay attention, learn, and function properly.

### I'm Ambidextrous! Isn't That Cool?

Have you ever tried to write your name with your non-dominant hand? It's pretty funny, right? And really challenging!

So when we see a person who is ambidextrous and can use both hands equally to do things, it seems pretty amazing. In baseball, switch-hitters (players who can bat either right-handed or left-handed) are in demand.

But . . . when it comes to reading and writing, being ambidextrous is often a deterrent and a symptom of a learning problem. It is an indication that the student has difficulty crossing the midline of his or her body.

The two hemispheres of the brain are used for different tasks and process information differently. Establishing hand dominance appears to support the developing brain's hemispheric specialization. Being naturally ambidextrous has been found to be associated with academic challenges and difficulties with attention, memory, and logical reasoning.

## Tippy Toes and Learning Challenges

Starbucks is one of my favorite writing spots because: (1) it's acceptable to sit there alone with your computer, and (2) there are no interruptions. And, okay, (3) I like the drinks!

So I was sitting at Starbucks one day when two different families came in with their toddler boys who were almost exactly the same height and age (tiny, adorable, and about two years old). Both were wearing cute little tennis shoes.

What caught my attention was that one of the little boys was walking completely on his toes. He wasn't playing. He was just holding his dad's hand, walking along on tiptoe. The other little boy was walking by his mom with a typical heel-to-toe gait.

**Which of these little guys is more likely to have learning problems?**

Answer: The toddler on tiptoe.

Toe walking is not necessarily something to be alarmed about, and in many cases, it goes away all on its own, but according to Expert Answers on BabyCenter.com: "Toe walking with no accompanying physical problems is called *idiopathic toe walking*, and is frequently seen in children with language or other developmental disorders, though we don't know just why."

**Actually, we do have an idea why...**

Toe walking is a symptom of a retained primitive reflex –the Tonic Labyrinthine Reflex (TLR). This reflex becomes active at birth and integrates, or quits firing, because it is no longer needed at four to six months of age. It plays a vital role in developing the correct alignment of the head with the rest of the body. This is necessary for balance, eye tracking, auditory processing, muscle tone, and organized movements—all of which are essential to the development of our ability to focus, pay attention, and learn.

Some possible long-term effects of an unintegrated TLR are:

- Difficulty following verbal directions
- ADD/ADHD
- Poor reading comprehension
- Letter reversals
- Trouble copying from board
- Disorganization
- Forgetfulness
- Speech and language problems
- Balance and coordination difficulties
- Hunched posture
- Toe walking

We see many children and teens at Stowell Learning Center who have retained primitive reflexes contributing to their challenges with attention and learning. By using specific movement exercises and/or low level laser therapy techniques, these reflexes can be integrated, allowing students to be calmer, less anxious, more attentive, and more mentally available for learning.

Integrating the reflexes won't teach a struggling learner to read or do math, but with the removal of the neurological interference caused by retained reflexes, the remediation of academic skills goes more quickly and easily and sticks!

## Fright, Fight, or Flight

I remember going to a haunted house on Halloween when I was in the sixth grade. At one point, we were given peeled grapes in the dark and told that they were eyeballs. It was so deliciously creepy!

What is it about that little thrill of fear that is so fun? Maybe it's that we get to experience that little adrenaline rush while knowing deep down that the fear is temporary and not real.

Fear causes our senses to elevate to high alert: Our pupils get large to take in as much light as possible. Our ears become hypersensitive to sound. Our sense of touch is heightened. This is survival mode. When we are afraid, our survival mechanisms kick in.

A little self-induced fright on Halloween is fun, but it is not a state that we want to live in, as it is not conducive to communication, learning, or general well-being.

In order to move comfortably through our world and function with ease and flow in our lives, the messages that are coming into the brain and being communicated between the brain and the body need to be clear, complete, and accurate.

At the most basic level, much of the communication flowing between the brain and body via our nervous system happens as a result of reflexes. Unintegrated reflexes create glitches in that communication.

Getting clear, accurate, and complete information through our tactile, auditory, and visual processing systems and being able to quickly comprehend and connect what we are experiencing with what we already know helps us to function and move through our environment and relationships securely. If the information from these sensory systems is not being received or perceived accurately, it can lead to anxiety, depression, illness, fearfulness, lack of confidence, and a myriad of learning or attention challenges.

## Got Rhythm?
### *Rhythm and timing may be a factor in reading, attention, and learning problems*

Have you ever taken one of those whole-body workout classes? I think it should be called *whole body–whole brain workout* because it not only takes muscle power, but also brainpower to coordinate all the simultaneous movements: arms opening and closing, twisting hand weights toward the center and then out to the side while sitting and tightening the abs and alternately flexing and pointing the feet. Yikes!

What I've noticed is that if I'm on the beat, everything seems to flow and work, but if I can't quite coordinate the rhythm, it all falls apart. I feel confused and lost, and a little overwhelmed. I try to get the feet going right but then lose track of what the arms are supposed to be doing. I start looking at the clock, wondering how much longer the class is. I may stop and give up on that part or realize that the instructor has gone on to something else, and now I'm behind.

Sound familiar? Struggling students experience these feelings every day.

# TAKE THE STONE OUT OF THE SHOE

Timing is at the most basic foundation of nearly everything we do. When timing is intrinsic and automatic, everything flows and functions better. Anything that requires coordination requires a sense of timing and rhythm; in other words, just about everything.

- Getting out of bed in the morning
- Eating
- Brushing teeth
- Walking, running, playing, and sports
- Speaking with intonation and expression
- Turn-taking and dialogue
- Handwriting
- Listening
- Processing speech sounds for phonetic decoding and reading
- Seeing letters, words, and sentences properly on the page
- Reading fluency
- Understanding what you hear and read
- Getting and responding to information quickly
- Retrieving and quickly organizing the words you want to say
- Organizing
- Planning and scheduling
- Regulating our breath, attention, and behavior

According to Advanced Brain Technologies,[4] "Neuroscience has proven through functional brain imaging that music engages more brain areas than anything else, and rhythm is the most important and fundamental aspect of music. Your brain health and body–brain connection depend on rhythm."

Dyslexic learners often have neuro-timing deficits that cause them to experience confusion and disorientation when looking at a page of print.

Students with social challenges sometimes have timing issues that cause their speech to sound stilted and just a little off cadence and therefore different and difficult to understand.

Awkward, uncoordinated movements that keep kids from enjoying sports may be the result of poor rhythm and timing.

Timing is one of many underlying skills that support efficient learning. In our work with students with learning and attention challenges, we are finding that improving timing and rhythm:

- Improves attention, coordination, and overall mental alertness for learning
- Reduces anxiety and improves behavior
- Increases speech, language, and verbal flow and expression

Feeling in sync feels good. One of the reasons teens traditionally gravitate toward music with a strong beat is because there is so much going on in a teenage brain and body that a strong beat is calming to their system.

## I'm Not Being a Wild Child on Purpose!

Most of the time, parents bring their kids to us because they're struggling with reading, math, or some other aspect of school. But because the underlying skills that are needed for easy, efficient learning are the same skills that support behavior, attention, social skills, and overall functioning, our students and families experience many life changes in addition to their academics.

I just have to share a couple of stories parents shared with me that made my day!

### *No more wedding craziness!*

In (happy) tears, Pete's mom said, "I don't know what you're doing, but it's working! Pete is so much calmer. Last week we went to a wedding, and he was still a kid but in control instead of being a wild child. I didn't have to say, 'Sit down! Stop! Don't embarrass me!'"

Pete wasn't being a "wild child" on purpose. Once his underlying learning skills (sensorimotor integration, auditory processing, spatial awareness and orientation) started to improve, he started feeling more confident, reading better, and was able to feel more settled and in control. This made everyone's life easier.

### *Happy mom! Happy family! Happy life!*

A teacher and one of our parents shared this story:

"I'm lying down with Aidan as we tell bedtime stories. Hard to imagine a year ago we didn't snuggle like this. His sensory processing disorder made snuggling uncomfortable for him. Now he's resting his head on me and going on about good guys (or Ninja Turtles) saving the day from the Naughty Man & his robots. And when I kiss him, he doesn't pull away anymore. (For the record, we have never let him watch a Ninja Turtle show, but he seems to know all about them). I don't care how silly his stories get, I appreciate how bright he is and the fact we can cuddle like I know other parents do with their kids. Aidan has a long way to go, but the improvement in one year is so astounding I have to remind myself how hard it was last year when we have a difficult moment today. Happy mom! Happy family! Happy life!"

## Understanding Students with Sensory Processing Disorder (SPD)

### Sensory traffic jam

If you live near a big city, you know all about traffic jams. A. Jean Ayres, a pioneer in the field of sensory integration, talked about *sensory processing disorder* (SPD) (formerly *sensory integration dysfunction*) as being like a traffic jam that prevents certain parts of the brain from receiving the information needed to interpret input from the body or the environment correctly.

With SPD, the brain has difficulty receiving and accurately interpreting information from the senses. It is as though the information comes in and then gets mixed up so that it doesn't get organized into an appropriate action or response.

The unexpected, confusing responses of students with SPD are often misinterpreted as bad behavior or ADHD. The students themselves may experience anxiety and low self-esteem as their own unreliable perceptions and responses disrupt their daily lives.

### Sensory overload

It is not uncommon for anyone to experience sensory

overload once in a while, but for the student with sensory processing disorder, hypersensitivity can be a constant disruption and source of overwhelm.

Austin, a thirteen-year-old student, shared that typical classroom noises–writing with a pencil, feet–shuffling, the ruffle of papers–made it almost impossible for him to function. He said that it was like the noises were "screaming" in his head.

Sensory overload puts us in a state of fight or flight, literally. Your overloaded SPD child may run, hide, or shut down (flight), or she may have meltdowns, tantrums, or get aggressive (fight). In Austin's case, it was flight. He ended up at the nurse's office most days, asking to go home.

### *What does SPD look like at school?*

Sensory processing difficulties look different for every child. They may involve one or multiple senses. At different times, students may be hyper or hyposensitive. They may not be able to discriminate sensation such as pain, hot, or cold adequately.

Here are some characteristics often seen in students with sensory processing disorder:

- Confused or clumsy in everyday tasks
- Overwhelmed during passing periods or in the cafeteria
- Have a tendency to chew on their clothing
- Unable to gage pencil pressure, so writing is wispy or may constantly break their pencil point
- Unaware of own strength or may use too much muscle. For example, they may push someone when

they meant to touch the person's shoulder, or rip the page when trying to turn it.
- Makes poor eye contact – may need to look away or block off visual stimuli in order to listen
- Unaware of other people's space
- Constantly moving, bumping into things, and seeming out of control
- Hates finger painting or anything slimy or sticky
- Agitated by smells (perfume, soap, the smell of the locker room)
- Excessively startled by loud noises
- Irritated by bright light
- Appears to over-react or under-react

As with other learning differences and attention challenges, addressing the underlying skills at the root of the problem can permanently change the effects of SPD.

Debra, a teacher and parent of an eleven-year-old with SPD, shared that before starting cognitive educational therapy at the Learning Center, everyone on the school IEP team was concerned about her son's motivation and social skills.

After therapy, she said, "Every single school personnel said two of his strengths were his motivation and his social skills. I just started crying. We've seen the academic growth, which is awesome, but those two things, that's immeasurable!"

[4] Advanced Brain Technologies (ABT) has researched and developed neuroscience-based music programs including TLP (The Listening Program) to help people achieve optimal brain health.

Chapter Five
# WHAT DO CHALLENGES WITH PROCESSING SKILLS LOOK LIKE?

## Challenges at the Processing Skills Level

These are skills such as attention, memory, auditory and visual processing, processing speed, language comprehension, and phonological awareness. Problems in this area may show up as:

- Trouble sounding out words
- Slow or poor reading
- Trouble memorizing spelling words or math facts
- Ability to read but inability to remember or understand what was read
- Fatigue from listening
- Missing information when listening
- Trouble understanding visual organization in math, charts, etc.
- Disorientation when reading, writing, or listening
- Ability to learn words for spelling tests but inability to remember the next week
- Poor attention

- Ability to do the work but inability to get it together to get the work done and turned in
- Slow work/working too hard or too long

### Auditory Processing Problems Are Like Listening Underwater

From the time I was twelve, I spent virtually every day of the summer hanging out or lifeguarding at the high school pool. Even now, the smell of chlorine at a pool brings back fond memories.

If you're an underwater swimmer, you know that sounds are very muffled under the surface of the water.

One mom that I spoke with recently shared that she always believed that the way her son heard was like listening underwater. Can you imagine the effect this would have on someone's speech and learning?

This boy's hearing had been tested every year and was always normal, but his speech was extremely unclear, and his reading and comprehension were extremely delayed. He had had continuous ear infections through the age of three, causing him to literally be listening through fluid.

In spite of the fact that his ears were working and he could hear, his ability to accurately perceive and process what he heard (auditory processing) was extremely weak. As a result, his brain was not "hearing" or processing the sounds in words clearly and accurately, causing his speech to be unintelligible and leaving him with a reading problem that wouldn't be resolved with more reading practice.

If someone is trying to speak to you underwater, the best solution to the problem of not understanding is for both of you to come out of the water. The best solution to "hearing through water" because of an auditory processing problem is stimulating and developing the brain's auditory processing system.

The auditory system is a dynamic system that *can* be stimulated and retrained. It's amazing to see what happens for students when the brain is getting clear, complete, and accurate information to think with. With auditory stimulation and specific instruction in listening, speaking, reading, and/or comprehension, children and adults with these challenges can become articulate speakers and readers.

## Why Isn't Everybody Talking about Auditory Processing?

I am continually astounded when I hear from many speech/language therapists and reading specialists that they know little to nothing about auditory processing. How can that be when auditory processing is the very foundation of language and reading?

Speaking, reading, and other academic skills are like the branches and leaves of a tree. They are the most obvious, noticeable part. But a tree will not survive without a good root system and trunk to carry the nutrients.

Learning of any kind also needs a "root system and trunk." The information coming in through the senses has to be perceived, processed, and organized correctly in order to use it for learning. In the case of both language and reading, the root system or foundation is auditory processing.

## *It's hard to get the message when you have a bad connection*

Perhaps the best way to understand the ramifications of an auditory processing problem is to think about what it is like to be in an important conversation with a bad cell phone connection. You find yourself having to listen extremely hard, and any extra noise around you becomes irritating and hard to block out.

Because the signal is not clear, you miss part of what the speaker is saying, and you find yourself saying, "What did you say?" and struggling to fill in the gaps.

You're not exactly sure what the speaker said, but you don't want to sound stupid or uninterested, so you make what you think is an appropriate response. When that backfires, because you respond incorrectly or inappropriately, you have to explain about the bad connection and why you misinterpreted what they said.

It takes so much energy to keep up with this conversation that you find your attention drifting. You feel distracted and frustrated, and important conversation or not, you just want to get off the phone!

Luckily for cell phone users, the way to a better connection is to hang up and try again.

But for students with auditory processing challenges, this is life. Poor or inconsistent auditory input can affect, among other things, the following:

- Listening
- Following directions

- Comprehension
- Memory
- Attention
- Reading
- Spelling
- Articulation and pronunciation
- Vocabulary
- Conversation and social skills
- Intonation and verbal expression
- Sense of well-being

Children and adults with auditory processing challenges may find listening exhausting and simply cannot keep it up for long. As a result, they may look unmotivated or like they have attention deficit. They may feel lost and anxious.

Reading and spelling have a direct correlation to *phonological awareness*–the auditory processing skill that allows the person to think about the number, order, and identity of sounds inside of words and the sound groupings that make up common patterns in the language.

When students are struggling to speak clearly and accurately, use appropriate intonation, express themselves verbally, or read, spell, or comprehend, the first place to explore is auditory processing.

Remediation of specific speech, language, and reading skills is important, but if the underlying processing/learning skills that are causing the problem are not addressed as well, the student will most likely never become as efficient and comfortable a learner as he or she could be.

## The Listening–Learning Connection

> If you're not listening, you're not learning.
> *–Lyndon Baines Johnson*

I think this is a pretty profound statement. I realize there are many ways to learn, but our experience with thousands of children and adults with learning challenges has shown that the vast majority of individuals who struggle with learning, including dyslexia and attention challenges, have difficulties with auditory processing or listening.

Living with an auditory processing delay or a weakness with listening skills can be fatiguing and frustrating. The ear has neurological connections to nearly every organ and function in the body as well as the attention, emotional, language, and learning centers in the brain. As a result, poor listening skills can cause a person to experience difficulties with speaking, reading, spelling, comprehension, attention, communication, energy, and sense of well-being.

Good listening/auditory skills depend upon being able to take in and process a very broad range of sound frequencies. When the brain is not processing the full range of frequencies, the listener may get incomplete and inaccurate information.

Individuals with weak auditory processing may do some or all of the following:

- Miss details or parts of what was said
- Mishear and therefore misunderstand or misinterpret information
- Confuse similar-sounding words
- Have trouble sounding out or pronouncing words
- Feel lost and confused

- Feel anxious
- Look like they are not paying attention
- Have poor attention when listening
- Give responses that don't match the question or conversation
- Withdraw or talk incessantly so that they don't have to listen

### Symptoms of auditory processing delay

Does your child do the following:

- Say, "Huh?" "What?" frequently? Often ask for things to be repeated?
- Have normal hearing acuity but an inconsistent response to auditory stimuli?
- Have difficulty following oral directions?
- Seem to have a short attention span?
- Fatigue easily during auditory (listening) tasks?
- Have poor long-term and short-term memory?
- Look at you when you're speaking but not appear to be listening?
- Have trouble listening when there is background noise?
- Have difficulty determining where a sound is coming from?
- Have difficulty with phonics, reading, or spelling?
- Have mild speech or articulation problems?
- Have disruptive behaviors (distracted, impulsive, frustrated)?
- Often feel anxious or lost?

- Have a history of ear infections?

These are symptoms of weak auditory processing skills and auditory processing disorder.

### Auditory processing challenges misdiagnosed

Auditory processing has a profound impact on learning and behavior, but so often, it is not recognized as being the source of the problem.

My daughter and son both travel extensively for their jobs. When they are overseas and we speak to them, the connection is often very poor–cutting in and out. As a result, listening and conversation become extremely taxing. We try hard to piece together what each other are saying, but we find that we lose both attention and comprehension. Conversations can become frustrating and even irritating.

It is obvious when a Skype or cell phone signal is bad, but very difficult to discern when the signal or message that the brain is getting in normal listening is compromised or confusing. Attention drifts are often associated with an attention deficit. Poor comprehension and direction following are seen as attention or motivation problems. Frustration, anxiety, and social challenges caused by poor listening skills are often viewed as psychological or emotional issues.

Reading problems almost always have auditory processing challenges at the root–at least in part. Research tells us that a set of auditory skills called *phonological awareness* is the greatest predictor of success or failure in reading.[5] Phonological awareness is the brain's ability to think about and manipulate the sounds and syllables in words. Without this ability, our phonetic language does not make sense.

Learning difficulties and struggles in school and/or social situations are most often the result of weak or inconsistent learning skills. These underlying skills cause interference in learning. Auditory processing skills are some of these underlying skills.

Unfortunately, these skills do not typically improve with time or traditional tutoring. However, through the use of specifically targeted sound therapy and auditory stimulation and training exercises, the brain can be retrained to perceive and use auditory information more completely, easily, and accurately.

## The Listening–Emotional/Social Connection

One evening, we did a special event for our students: SLC Science Lab–a.k.a. Big Fun Mess and Parents' Night Out.

Only one of four experiments worked exactly as planned, but the night was a big success.

The students had a good time working together to make a liquid kaleidoscope and homemade Silly Putty, Play-Doh, and lip balm. While some of our students are social butterflies, others are not so skilled. Parents and staff loved seeing all the students getting a chance to laugh and be social.

People are social creatures. Listening skills have a huge impact on our success or failure socially. Listening is different than hearing. Hearing is what our ears do, but listening is intentional. It involves intentional attention.

Our brain looks for patterns. The emotional part of the brain helps us pick out the important patterns in the sound around us and sends it to several places in the brain so it can be processed. In order to do this quickly, the brain must filter out the unimportant information.

Students who struggle socially may actually be experiencing a failure of the brain's inhibitory response–or filtering of unimportant sound. As a result, they "hear" everything and cannot quickly focus on what's important in order to give the expected response. They may become overloaded and shut down. They may learn not to participate because they can't keep up in conversations or discussions, causing them to say the wrong thing or get laughed at. With extreme overload, they may respond by running away, screaming, making loud noises, or covering their ears. These survival responses don't endear them to their peers and make friendships difficult.

Auditory processing and listening skills can be developed. The brain can be retrained to process sound more effectively so that students can learn and function in both social and academic environments more comfortably, appropriately, and independently.

### Agh! My Teacher Talks Too Fast!
*The impact of slow processing speed*

Students with learning challenges sometimes feel like their teacher is talking at breakneck speed. They're trying hard to listen, they're looking at the teacher, but somehow, the teacher is already onto the next question when the student has just barely come up with a response to the last one.

When a question is asked, most people automatically understand the question and begin thinking about and formulating their response. Students with language-based learning disabilities often struggle to process the *question* as well as the answer. While they are deciphering the sequence of words, grammar, vocabulary, and intention behind the question, someone else has already answered it. When they are ready to respond, the teacher has gone on to the next question, and they've missed it.

What does that look like in the classroom? It looks like a student who isn't paying attention or isn't listening.

We worked with a bright and talkative twelve-year-old who constantly repeated what someone else had just said in discussions or asked questions that the teacher had just answered. After the first few weeks in sixth grade, he learned not to participate because he was always saying the wrong thing, and everyone but him seemed to know it. He just knew the other kids laughed and he was always being told to pay attention.

But attention wasn't the problem. The problem was, by the time he had processed the question and come up with an answer, the question had been answered and the class had gone on to the next one . . . and he'd missed it.

I remember testing a high school student who either said "I don't know" or gave really off-the-wall responses to virtually every test question. Then I realized that he had such slow auditory processing speed that any responses he gave were actually correct answers to *previous* questions. And that was in a one-to-one setting. I can't imagine how lost he must have felt in the classroom. His parents and teachers thought he just didn't try and didn't care. Of course he had a bad attitude! He had no idea what was going on in real time!

## "I Don't Get It. What Do You Mean?"
### *A look at comprehension challenges*

My daughter has learned that volunteering to wait for the next flight when hers is overbooked is a good way to add to her travel funds. And since she has an insatiable desire to travel, she makes a habit of asking.

Once when flying home from Japan, she texted me this exchange with the airline agent:

My daughter: Hello, Is the flight overbooked today?

Lady: Yes. Overbooked.

My daughter: Do you need volunteers?

Lady:

I laughed so hard! I could just picture the scene and the airline agent cocking her head to the side, thinking, "What is this crazy American talking about?"

This "confused baby" picture was making the rounds on social media at the time. His look of "Huh? I have no idea what you mean," is adorable! But for students trying to understand a lesson in class or study for a test, that feeling of complete confusion is not much fun.

Comprehension challenges are tricky because they are often very subtle. On the surface, these students seem to use and understand language like everyone else, but they may struggle with relationships, humor, and people's intention and may tend to be quite literal in their take on things. They may appear to have attention problems because they miss details, misinterpret what people say, and lose their focus when listening or reading. The brain will quit paying attention to something that just doesn't make sense.

Just as with any other learning challenge, making real and permanent changes in comprehension requires identifying and developing the lagging underlying learning/processing skills—skills such as auditory processing, working memory, long-term memory, visual attention, visualization, and reasoning.

## HAPPY HOLIDAYS *Form, Johnny*
## *The impact of visual processing challenges*

"Form" Johnny?

In order to be a good speller, you have to be able to hold an accurate mental picture of words in your mind. You also have to understand the sound system of our language, but without a clear mental image (a visual processing skill), it becomes very difficult to catch and correct your errors.

### *Visual processing*

A tremendous amount of information comes in through our visual system. The eye has neurological connections to nearly every organ and function in the body as well as the attention, emotional, and learning centers in the brain. Weak or inefficient processing of visual information can make reading and writing stressful and fatiguing.

Can you imagine how much effort and energy it would take to read if your brain paid more attention to the white spaces on the page than the letters? What if the page looked like this when you tried to read it?

**Mha tif baqe the lookeb lik eth is when you rtied ot reab? Wonld yon relaly waufto read? Moulb it make ony wanj ot try harber or jnst wnatto thorm the dook onutthe min dow?**

Visual processing affects a person's ability to understand the visual organization on the page needed for math and using charts, graphs, and tables. We once had a high school student in advanced placement (AP) classes who had no idea why a planner had days of the week across the top and times of day down the side. The visual organization of it was completely baffling to him. No wonder he refused to use it!

The highest level of visual processing is being able to visualize, manipulate, and think with mental images. Weaknesses in this area can affect comprehension, planning, problem-solving, and mental flexibility (seeing things from different perspectives and points of view).

Here's what a student with a visual-processing problem might look like at school (not all students have all symptoms):

- Has disorganized backpack or desk
- Can't find homework or materials
- Does messy work; uses lines and spacing poorly
- Has trouble copying from the board or book
- Reads slowly; gets sleepy when reading
- It disoriented when reading; refuses to read
- Skips items on tests/worksheets
- Doesn't notice parts of directions or assignments

- Can't locate where to look on the board or in the book
- Doesn't use a planner or calendar well, if at all
- Doesn't understand the organization/steps in math
- Doesn't line up numbers in math
- Has comprehension problems

Children and adults with visual processing problems may seem like underachievers who just aren't attentive or motivated enough. They frustrate themselves, parents, spouses, teachers, and coworkers because they procrastinate or refuse to do things that it seems like they should be able to do. The reality is that their avoidance and lack of visual attention are more likely related to confusion and discomfort than to stubbornness and lack of caring.

---

[5] Stanovich (1983) said that in the early stages of reading, phonological awareness is the strongest predictor of reading progress. Stanovich (1986, 1988, 1993) outlined a model in which problems with phonological skills early on lead to a downward spiral where even higher level cognitive skills are eventually affected by slow reading development.

Chapter Six
# WHAT DO CHALLENGES WITH EXECUTIVE FUNCTION LOOK LIKE?

## Challenges with Executive Function

Executive function is our personal manager that guides and directs our attention and behavior. It helps us reason, problem solve, organize, make decisions, and evaluate and modify our actions. Students with issues in this area may have the following issues:

- Poor time management
- Inability to organize materials
- Trouble reasoning
- Procrastination; waiting last minute to start studying for tests or work on a long-term assignment
- Inability to plan and organize projects
- Lack of tact
- Poor follow-through
- Trouble getting started
- Poor mental flexibility

## Is Poor Executive Function Getting Your Child in Trouble?

The bell rings. Eleven-year-old Kasey explodes from her desk and races out the door, knocking into a few desks, trampling a few toes, and elbowing several classmates out of the way. She is so ready for recess and trots off to grab a ball before anyone else does.

Kasey has no idea that there is a problem. After all, the bell rang, and all she's doing is going outside for recess! But once again, she is in trouble, and her parents are going to get a call because she knocked a classmate down as she jetted out the door.

Kasey is a nice, well-meaning kid, but she has very poor executive function skills. She is unable to self-monitor and manage her attention and behavior. She wouldn't purposely knock other students down, but she is impulsive and doesn't mentally predict or evaluate the consequences of her actions.

Executive function skills are high-level self-management skills that develop all the way through childhood, but don't completely develop until about age twenty-five. Most students need some guidance in developing executive function, and some, like Kasey, need a great deal of intentional, guided, and monitored instruction.

### HELP! My Kid Is Driving Me Crazy Because He…

- Is disorganized
- Never cleans his room
- Is always late
- Avoids getting started on homework

- Puts school projects off until the last minute
- Has no sense of time
- Refuses to write down his assignments in his planner
- Doesn't care about his work and just rushes to get it done

## Executive function: the self-management system of the brain

Executive function skills are self-management skills that, among other things, involve strategizing, organizing, planning, evaluating, reasoning, and monitoring and managing one's own attention and behavior.

Executive function skills are critical for health, growth, and development academically, socially, and psychologically. The three core executive functions are:

- **Working memory** (mentally holding information while working with it)
- **Inhibitory control** (self-control over attention, behavior, thoughts, and emotions)
- **Cognitive flexibility** (adjusting to change and ability to see things in different ways)

Executive function skills develop slowly over time and well into the twenties, but are critical for smooth sailing at every age.

## Does my child have an executive function disorder?

If underlying learning/processing skills are in place and the student actually *can* do the work, poor executive function may be the culprit if the student has chronic difficulties executing daily tasks such as the following:

- Organizing materials
- Setting schedules
- Keeping room, desk, and backpack organized
- Getting started
- Staying focused on necessary tasks
- Sustaining effort to finish tasks

The student might also have issues with the following:

- Misplacing papers, school assignments, and other school materials
- Losing or forgetting where they put personal items
- Seeming lazy or unmotivated because they can do the work but don't

Executive function challenges also show up in the student's ability to manage emotions and social relationships. Students may show signs of the following:

- Difficulty holding off instead of impulsively jumping in to say or do something
- Not seeming to learn from their mistakes
- Hurting others' feelings because they didn't evaluate the consequences of their words
- Having trouble shifting mentally or emotionally to think about something or try something in a different way
- Seeming to fall short no matter how hard they try

## ADHD–I'm Not Losing Focus on Purpose!

As a teacher, what do you tell the parent of a child who is smart, delightful, and completely out to lunch in class–physically there but not mentally present? Or physically all over the place–standing up, sitting down, touching everyone and everything?

When you can't keep your body in one place, when you notice absolutely everything around you, when your mind is racing so fast that you miss most of what is said to you by a parent or teacher, it's pretty hard to focus on schoolwork or show how smart you really are.

Attention challenges are often the result of weak neurodevelopmental or Core Learning Skills. When primitive reflexes are retained, they can cause neurological interference, like roadblocks, to efficient learning and functioning. They can also create tremendous stress on the attention system.

Many attention challenges are the symptoms of stressed underlying processing skills rather than the actual root of the problem. A person with weak auditory, visual, or language skills will struggle to get clear and accurate information when listening or reading. Imagine how hard it would be to pay attention if:

- Most of what you heard sounded like you were on a bad cell phone connection
- The words on the page seemed to move around, or
- It felt like you were listening to or reading a foreign language that you didn't really understand when listening or reading.

But . . . sometimes the root of the attention problem is attention. In my opinion, far too many students get diagnosed as having attention deficit/hyperactivity disorder (ADHD)–students who actually have underdeveloped skills at the Core Learning or Processing Skills levels of the Learning Skills Continuum. However, experience with thousands of students with attention challenges has shown us that ADHD is real and can be the root of the student's under-performance at school and in other areas of their life.

ADHD impacts approximately 11 percent of school-age students. These students tend to have inappropriate levels of inattention, impulsivity, and sometimes hyperactivity for their age. ADHD represents a delay in development of executive function skills. When students don't develop internal control, they become needy and attention seeking and have a lack of self-regulation.

Biochemistry is often a factor in ADHD. When that is the case, the solution will usually need to include a biochemical intervention (medication, supplements, and/or diet) and specific attention and executive function training.

## Multitasking or Scattered and Unfocused?
*Is social media helping or hurting attention and executive function?*

Have you watched a high school or college student do homework recently? It's quite a fantastic display of multitasking. Or is it?

I am amazed at how young people can switch so rapidly between texting and all the social media platforms, all while doing an assignment or studying for a test. Is this a coordinated multitasking skill, or is it actually more related to a scattered, unfocused mind?

I am not against technology. In fact, like everyone else these days, I have no idea how I could live without it, but it does have its drawbacks. I believe one of those is making us think that being glued to a video game for hours at a time is an example of sustained focus, or that carrying on multiple interactions in a variety of social media platforms is a coordinated multitasking skill.

Many parents come to Stowell Learning Centers with concerns about their child or teen's executive function skills. Executive function is the CEO part of the brain that allows a person to monitor, control, and evaluate his or her own attention and behavior. Our executive function allows us to organize time and materials, solve problems, make decisions, and delay gratification.

Multimedia multitasking may be impressive, but a far better example of good executive function would be the student who turns off all social media while studying and puts their complete focus and attention on the single task at hand.

Chapter Seven
# RECOGNIZING CHALLENGES WITH DYSLEXIA, DYSGRAPHIA, DYSCALCULIA, AND BASIC ACADEMICS

## Is My Child Dyslexic?

Dyslexia is coming to the forefront as more and more states are looking at legislation around dyslexia and education.

Most sources now site 15–20 percent of students as being dyslexic. Here are some questions parents should ask that will help them determine if dyslexia testing is warranted:

- Is there a family history of dyslexia?
- Was there difficulty learning the alphabet?
- Is there lingering difficulty with letter and number reversals, particularly after age seven?
- Does the student have difficulty sounding out unfamiliar words?
- Does he or she tend to add, omit, shift, repeat, or substitute sounds in words when reading, spelling, or speaking?
- Does the student have average to above-average intelligence?

- Does the student have talents in non-academic areas (sports, acting, music, art, mechanics)?
- Does the student tend to be creative or artistic? Good at building things?
- Does the student see things in a different way? Think outside the box?
- Does the student tend to get very frustrated with himself over his reading and writing challenges, calling himself stupid or dumb?

All of these are very common characteristics of dyslexia.

## Recognizing the dyslexic learner at different grade levels

**K–1:** We never want to mistake developmental youngness for dyslexia and age five and a half is the peak age for letter reversals and inversions. However, our very young dyslexic students show much greater than normal struggles with recognizing and writing the alphabet. Not only do they have many more letter and number reversals, but also they tend to leave out letters when saying or writing the alphabet and often have to sing the alphabet in order to think about individual letters. They tend to perceive *l*, *m*, *n*, *o* as one entity: "elemeno."

**Primary grades:** Dyslexic learners are generally quite bright and often have very good comprehension. If they also have good language and memory skills, they may be able to memorize the stories–especially in first or second grade. They can fool teachers and parents into thinking that they can read.

**Upper grades:** Somewhere between third and sixth grades, the reading and writing demands have increased to the point that the dyslexic student can no longer keep up. Some work excessively hard and long to get the work done; others begin to look lazy and unmotivated.

At this age, there will be residual evidence of reversals, but students may have learned to consciously think about every *b* or *d* that they see or want to write, so they self-correct or avoid making those errors. Their writing will often reflect very poor spacing, difficulty forming legible letters, and serious spelling challenges.

These students will drag out their homework in an attempt to avoid the stress of reading and writing. They may hate reading by this point, or may read only what they are interested in. This confuses people into thinking that they can read well, when the reality is that they are grabbing content words and filling in the gaps with what they know about the story or subject already.

**Middle school/high school:** These students may be pegged as lazy because they often have good thoughts and ideas to contribute in oral discussions, but have written expression that is far below par. Unknowingly even to themselves, this is likely because they are writing with words they can spell, causing their writing to be short and simplistic.

Dyslexic students who have good listening and comprehension skills can learn a great deal from class lectures but take terrible notes and do poorly on tests where they actually have to read the questions accurately. In groups, they may become very adept at getting others to do the writing.

### What do dyslexic reading challenges look like?

Dyslexia has both visual and auditory components and varying degrees of severity. Here are some specific symptoms often seen in dyslexic readers:

- Sound out words letter by letter, but blend the sounds together incorrectly

- Add, omit, shift, repeat, or substitute sounds in words when reading
- Many false starts and self-corrections because decoding is unstable
- Know phonetic rules (such as the silent *e* at the end of words) but can't consistently apply them
- Confuse visually similar words such as *quietly* and *quickly*
- Read very fast, slurring or mumbling through words they don't know
- Sound like they are reading well but are not reading the words on the page, making up their own context or filling in the gaps with what makes sense to them
- Repeat words, phrases, and sentences often to make it sound right or to catch the meaning
- Add, change, move, or omit small common sight words such as *the*, *of*, and *a*
- Struggle painfully through each sound and word
- Hate to read orally and show avoidance behaviors when have to read (cry, talk, act out, get a stomachache, refuse)
- Recognize difficult content words (such as *elephant*) but miss easy words

### *Prognosis for dyslexia*

It is commonly believed that dyslexia is a life-long struggle, to be coped with but never to be corrected. Neuroscience research proves that through targeted and intensive cognitive training, the brain can rewire itself to learn to process information more effectively.

We have absolutely found this to be true! Dyslexic learners can become good readers and spellers. More reading will not do the trick, but identifying and correcting the weak underlying skills and then intentionally and sequentially remediating the reading and spelling skills will.

## What Do Dyslexic Spelling Challenges Look Like?

When parents of dyslexic students describe their child's spelling, they often use words like *horrible* and *atrocious*. Spelling can be even trickier for dyslexic students than reading, because they cannot rely on context and comprehension to help them figure out the words.

Spelling difficulties will vary depending upon the type of dyslexic challenges[6] the student has:

- **Dysnemkinesia** (difficulty remembering and writing letter symbols without reversals)
- **Dysphonesia** (difficulty connecting sound and symbol in order to use phonics for reading and spelling)
- **Dyseidesia** (difficulty visually recognizing whole words for reading and recalling the visual image for spelling)

Most often, students have some **combination** of these dyslexic types. Here are some common symptoms of spelling challenges that we see with our dyslexic students:

- Memorize words for the test but cannot retain them later
- Miss words they knew in order on the list when given in a different order on the test

- Write words that are completely undecipherable because the sounds and letters make no sense to them
- Transpose letters or write letters in a generic way because they aren't really sure what the letter looks like or what letter actually goes in there
- Add, omit, repeat, shift, or substitute sounds in words (phonological awareness errors)
- Write a continuous stream of letters with no or erratic spacing when writing
- Draw the letters
- Spell phonetically
- Leave out vowels
- Remember some of the important letters in sight words but put them in the wrong place or sequence in the word
- Omit endings

## Dysgraphia Basics

Students with dysgraphia may have difficulty with the physical writing process as well as getting their ideas from head to paper. Writing requires a complex combination of visual, motor, language, and cognitive processing skills, so just like dyslexia, *dysgraphia* is a fairly broad term with many subtypes and each dysgraphic learner is unique.

### *Common characteristics*

- Too tight or too light pencil grip and pressure
- Awkward or unusual wrist, body, or paper position when writing
- Poor spacing of margins, words, and letters on the page

- Frequent erasing
- Poor spelling, including unfinished words or missing words or letters
- Slower writing than typical same-age students
- Mixed upper and lowercase letters when writing words and sentences
- Irregular and inconsistent letter formation, size, spacing, and placement
- Reversal of letters and numbers
- Avoidance of writing tasks
- Difficulty with written organization and expression even though they may have good ideas when speaking

Students with dysgraphia can be confusing to parents and teachers who see that "he can write neatly when he wants to." The truth is that if they very slowly and carefully *draw* the letters, these students may be able to produce a fairly neat and legible product. This is effortful, not sustainable, and not the same as writing with fluency.

Handwriting requires kinesthetic feedback in order to guide the hand and body to make the adjustments needed to apply appropriate pencil pressure and to write with accuracy and ease. Students with dysgraphia are often not getting enough kinesthetic feedback.

Numerous visual skills, including visual–spatial awareness, eye-hand coordination, and visual memory, are involved in spelling and writing. Difficulties with any of these skills draw mental attention away from the content and impact legibility.

Some students have difficulty crossing the vertical midline of their body. In order to avoid having to cross the midline, students may adopt very unusual and uncomfortable postures or positions and change the angle of the paper as they write. Their thoughts may be disrupted each time their hand has to cross the midline as their pencil moves from left to right across the page.

In spite of the fact that they have good ideas and can verbally express themselves well, some students with dysgraphia may experience a global interruption in the ability to get their thoughts from their head to the paper. This includes language organization, sequencing, spelling, grammar, sentence structure, and mechanics (such as capitalization and punctuation).

## Why Do Students Struggle with Math?

"Who, me? Do math? No way!"

People's reaction to math varies but often is quite emphatic and negative. What is it about math that makes even well-educated adults want to run and hide when their kids ask for help? What could be so intimidating about numbers?

We have found that many students try to learn math calculations and processes without really understanding what they are all about. As a result, they have inconsistent performance and are unable to catch and correct their errors. They never really understand how math works, so it becomes something to avoid.

Math is logical and provable. Everything about it makes sense if you understand how numbers work. Learning math by rote, without a foundation of understanding, does not work, at least not for very long.

We find that students with math difficulties often struggle with comprehension as well. They don't understand math vocabulary and cannot easily conceptualize the organization on the page or the logic of the processes.

### Underlying skills support success in math

A variety of skills contribute to math processing, including spatial awareness, visual attention to detail, visual numeric conceptualization (such as number line), symbol recognition and decoding, memory, sequential thinking, language comprehension, and reasoning.

### Identifying the real problem

When parents express concerns about math, we find that the real issue varies greatly. Students with dyscalculia truly do not have any idea how numbers work. Math has always been difficult for them. They cannot explain what they are doing, and their errors often seem completely random. It may look as though they aren't paying attention or don't care, but they truly don't get it.

Inability to memorize math facts is a huge concern of many parents and may be related to poor memory or attention skills coupled with a lack of context to place the facts in.

Particularly with the advent of Common Core curriculum in schools, more and more parents are reporting student difficulties with math. This seems to be related primarily to word problems. If students can do the computation but struggle once they are responsible for word problems, the issue may very well be a reading problem.

Weak ability to visualize and understand how the pieces fit into a whole can make math difficult for students. These students will typically have language comprehension problems as well.

Some students can do mental math but cannot show their work or do the math on paper. They understand the concepts and have the visual–spatial skills to think about numerical relations, but they have difficulty with symbols, sequential thinking, or visual organization on the page.

---

[6] Information and testing for the different types of dyslexia are found in the Dyslexia Determination Test Grades 2–12. Good-Lite (Formerly Richmond Products, Inc.).

Chapter Eight
# QUICK SCREENING TOOLS

### At-A-Glance Dyslexia Screener

This At-a-Glance Dyslexia Screener is a list of the most common functional characteristics of dyslexia seen with students based on Stowell Learning Center's extensive experience with evaluation and treatment for children and adults with dyslexia.

Dyslexia is likely, and further evaluation and training for dyslexia is recommended if you or your child, student, or patient experience difficult, slow, or laborious reading or spelling **and** any of the following:

\_\_\_\_\_ Family history of dyslexia

\_\_\_\_\_ Creative, visual–spatial thinking style–excels at arts, Legos, building, or sports

\_\_\_\_\_ Big-picture thinking; out-of-the-box ideas and problem-solving abilities

\_\_\_\_\_ High empathy, charisma, and/or social functioning

\_\_\_\_\_ Aversion to reading, but likes to be read to; strong comprehension abilities

_____ Difficulty learning the alphabet

_____ Lingering difficulty with letter and number reversals, particularly after age seven

_____ Difficulty sounding out unfamiliar words

_____ Frustration over reading and writing challenges

_____ Confusion with small common sight words such as *the, of,* and *if* when reading

_____ Bizarre or phonetic spelling; can memorize spelling words for test but can't retain

_____ Misreading of the word but getting the meaning (i.e. reading *cat* for *kitten*, or *house* for *home*)

_____ Writing with words they can spell; having much stronger oral expression than written

## Quick Learning Disability Screening Tool

These functional indicators of a learning disability are based on Stowell Learning Center's extensive experience with the evaluation and treatment of children and adults with diagnosed and undiagnosed learning disabilities.

If you or your child, student, or patient appear to have at least **average to above-average intelligence** and their life is being impacted by two or more of the following symptoms, they are experiencing a learning challenge, and further evaluation and training will be helpful in understanding and alleviating the difficulties.

### Risk Factors

_____ Family history of learning or attention challenges

_____ Early speech or language delay

_____ Born prematurely

_____ Born via C-Section

_____ Numerous ear infections

### Response to School

_____ Lacks confidence

_____ Works too hard or too long on homework

_____ Avoids school or homework

_____ Appears lazy or unmotivated

_____ Needs excessive help or reteaching; overly dependent

## Academic / Learning Struggles

\_\_\_\_\_ Trouble sounding out words

\_\_\_\_\_ Slow or poor reader

\_\_\_\_\_ Trouble memorizing spelling words or math facts

\_\_\_\_\_ Can read but can't remember or understand what was read

\_\_\_\_\_ Trouble organizing thoughts for speaking or writing

\_\_\_\_\_ Gets very tired when listening; misses information when listening

\_\_\_\_\_ Slow processing; delayed response

\_\_\_\_\_ Inconsistent performance

\_\_\_\_\_ Trouble understanding visual organization in math, charts, etc.

\_\_\_\_\_ Can learn words for spelling test but can't remember the next week

\_\_\_\_\_ Poor attention

\_\_\_\_\_ Can do the work but can't get it together to get the work done and turned in

\_\_\_\_\_ Slow work/working too hard or too long

## Quick Auditory Processing Screening Tool

These functional indicators of an auditory processing problem are based on Stowell Learning Center's extensive experience with evaluation and treatment for children and adults with learning or attention challenges related to auditory processing.

Weak, delayed, or inefficient auditory processing is likely when individuals consistently experience two or more of the following symptoms:

_____ Early speech, language, or articulation problems

_____ Constantly saying, "Huh?" or "What?" and needing things repeated

_____ Lip reading; watching speaker's mouth intently

_____ Feeling lost and confused when listening

_____ Losing attention in lectures and conversation even with good effort

_____ Being exhausted after a day at school, meetings, or social situations

_____ Mishearing or misunderstanding what is said to them

_____ Poor phonological awareness; difficulty with phonics, reading, or spelling

_____ Being overwhelmed by noisy environments

_____ Having trouble following a conversation in noise

At-a-Glance Screeners © 2021 Green Dot Press.
All Rights Reserved.
Developed by Jill Stowell, MS, Author, Learning Disability Specialist, Dislexia Remediation Specialist

# Part 2: Simple Strategies for Supporting Struggling Students

## *Introduction*

As soon as their child comes home from school with homework, parents are thrown into the role of teacher whether they have that skill set or not.

Teachers, with minimal to no special training on supporting students with learning differences or attention challenges, are expected to be experts in dealing with the needs of every student in their classroom.

Sometimes, a slight shift in language or mindset can make a huge difference for a struggling student. Simple strategies that support underlying processing skills can make learning easier, help students be more successful, and reduce the homework battles.

This section will give you practical, hands-on tools for supporting your struggling or underperforming student.

Chapter Nine
# GENERAL GUIDELINES

## Downtime Matters

Standing on the beach in one of my favorite spots in the world, Honokowai, Maui, I saw a giant sea turtle lazily sunning on the shore.

As I watched the turtle, it was a good reminder that no matter how structured or hectic life becomes, it's important to take a time out to breathe, to have even a few minutes of downtime.

When my kids were in school, it was hard as a busy mom to give myself even five minutes of downtime, but starting when my son was in kindergarten, I learned that he needed some quiet, unstructured time after school just to regroup before he could go on to anything else. A "lazy" few minutes can clear the mind–for kids and moms!

## Lessons from Dad
### #1 Dads like fun!

Many dads kid that they are just little boys at heart. They need their toys and playtime. There are some lessons to be learned there for students, especially those who struggle in school.

When school is difficult, it may not be a whole lot of fun for kids. They often miss recess or playtime at home just trying to get their work completed. Parents find it frustrating that their child won't just sit down and get their homework done rather than dragging it out all afternoon.

Maybe what the brain needs is a break - a little bit of fun, laughter, or movement – to re-energize it. Parents can structure Brain Breaks so that kids get the little reboot that they need without losing their momentum with homework. Try something like:

- If you have a basketball hoop, go outside and shoot (attempt) five baskets apiece
- Turn on music and do silly dances for five minutes
- Chase the dog around the yard for five minutes
- Play a five-minute game of UNO or some other quick, fun card game
- Have a Stacking Cups competition

These little Brain Breaks are a fun way to spend a few minutes together in a positive way, change attitudes, and increase energy. If a student knows he has a five-minute Brain Break to look forward to at the end of the task, it may increase his motivation and productivity. Please note

# TAKE THE STONE OUT OF THE SHOE

that these little breaks do not include screens. Movement can re-energize the brain for learning tasks. Devices will derail it.

### *#2: Boys need approval.*

Boys need approval. Little boys, big boys, boys who have grown up to be dads–they tend to be hard on themselves and operate best with approval. Boys won't generally play a game they don't think they can win, but they do like to play games.

Try breaking challenging tasks into small little competitions that the student can win:

- "We just did this stack of flashcards in two minutes. Let's do them one more time and see if you can beat your time!"
- "You got nine of these math facts correct last time, how many do you think you can get this time?"

### *#3: Validate the performance.*

- "When you wrote out this answer, your words gave me a really good mental picture!"
- "Wow! I think these three words are the stars of the page. They are so neat and easy to read!"
- "That was a good connection that you made between those two events in the story."
- "Asking your teacher to clarify the assignment shows maturity and that you are taking responsibility for your work. I'm really proud of you!"

Many of our boys won't take a compliment, but they feel proud of an accomplishment that is noted specifically. And that validation will encourage them to repeat it!

## Brain Break Activities to Get Unstuck, Refocused, and Restarted

At mile twenty of a twenty-one-mile bike ride, my husband and I stopped to take a little break. It had gotten warm, and we wanted to remove a few layers. When we started riding again, my legs let me know that enough was enough, and I thought, "I really don't want to ride anymore."

It made me think about a couple of students that we tested recently whose parents reported that their kids try so hard on their homework but have a terrible time coming back from a break. In fact, one of the students refused to take a break, saying, "I just won't do anything after a break."

You would think that after all their hard work, kids would welcome a break, and I'm sure they do, but when students have dyslexia, learning disabilities, attention deficits, or other struggles in school, the amount of effort, energy, and motivation they have to muster in order to do the task can be monumental. Building that back up again after a break can be daunting.

### *People need breaks. Brains need breaks.*

An overloaded brain is less productive, so periodic breaks are necessary for optimal performance, especially if what you are trying to do is as taxing as homework is for many of our struggling students.

As an employer, I am required to give my staff members breaks. So how do we give our kids a much-needed break without losing the focus, momentum, or determination we've worked so hard to establish?

### *Get unstuck with a built-in break*

Brain Breaks do not have to be as definitive as a coffee break or a play break, which for some students might completely reroute their focus and energy. They can be done without ever leaving the homework space and are a quick-and-easy way to revive attention, mental resources, and energy. They help students of any age **get unstuck**.

We work with students on **recognizing** when they need a Brain Break—when they feel too frustrated, sleepy, bored, emotional, or confused—and let them **choose** a brain break. Here are some Brain Breaks we suggest for students:

### *Five-Count Breath (3–5 times)*

- Inhale slowly through your nose and count to five on your fingers.
- Without holding your breath, begin exhaling slowly through your mouth in five counts as you put your fingers back down.

Deep breathing immediately forces oxygen into the brain, which improves thinking and encourages muscles to relax as they are flooded with oxygen-rich blood.

### *Palming (1–5 minutes)*

- Warm your hands by rubbing them together briskly.

- Gently place the heel of your hands over your eyes.
- Keep your neck and back straight, shoulders relaxed. Rest your elbows on the table.
- Breathe in and out slowly, feeling the warmth and darkness soothe the muscles of your eyes and whole body.

This is an excellent way to rest and refresh the mind and eyes.

### *Heart Breathing (1–5 minutes)*

- Place your attention on the area around your heart or center of the chest. It helps to put your hand over your heart area.
- Now pretend to breathe in and out of your heart. Take three slow breaths. (This is called *heart breathing*.)
- Think of someone or something that makes you smile or feel happy, like your mom or dad, your friends, or a special place you like to visit. Feel that happy feeling in your heart as you do your heart breathing.

This technique is good for reducing anxiety and increasing focus and attention.

### *Cross Crawls (1–2 minutes)*

- Touch hand or elbow to opposite knee, alternately moving one arm and opposite leg.

Cross Crawls activate the brain for reading, writing, and spelling and help students get unstuck.

### *Arm Swings (5–8 cycles)*

- Stand with your feet about 12–18 inches apart.
- Loosely swing your upper body and arms from side

to side. At the furthest point in the swing, look over your shoulder.
- Do 5–8 left-right cycles.

### *Breath Stretch (3–5 times)*

- Breathe in deeply through your nose as you bring your arms up above your head and come up on your toes. *Hold for a slow count of two.*

- Exhale through your mouth as you bring your arms down and come down off your toes.

All of us need Brain Breaks once in a while when we are working hard. Children and teens struggling with attention or learning may need these little breaks more often, as they are exerting much more energy than their peers to do the same task. Building Brain Breaks into your homework or learning session gives students the mental break they need in order to shift into a more productive and resourceful state without the trauma of coming back after a break.

These activities are also very effective to use before going to school or when starting homework, taking a test, or transitioning from one task to another.

### Laughter: A Good Attitude Adjuster!

Growing up, my children always loved visits from Aunt Nancy because she was so much fun. She would make them laugh, and they would do anything for her! Victor Borge said, "Laughter is the shortest distance between two people."

Laughter makes us feel good! Laughter supports our health. Laughter is just plain fun!

When students are starting to dig in because something is hard for them, I often find that being playful or kidding with them will adjust their attitude before it becomes a problem.

When my son was little, the last thing he wanted to do was study his reading flashcards. He was a very active little hockey player, and sitting and doing flashcards was torture. So I decided a little humor was needed.

Whenever we came to a word that was hard because it didn't follow the phonetic rules, I made a big show of tossing it over my shoulder and into the "penalty box" because it didn't follow the rules. Kevin would fall apart laughing. Such a silly little thing helped us get past the whining and through the flashcards with both of us in a better mood!

Students with learning challenges often experience a high degree of frustration and stress. A little laughter can really help lighten the mood and bring the brain back to a productive state.

For some kids, a little "tickle torture" will do the trick. A two-minute break to view a silly YouTube video can get the whole family laughing.

And, by the way, this is not just child's play! When you smile or laugh, feel-good chemicals are released in the brain: neuropeptides that help fight off stress; dopamine, which increases motivation, energy, and mood; endorphins, which act as a mild pain reliever; and serotonin, which is an antidepressant.

# TAKE THE STONE OUT OF THE SHOE

## 5 Tips for Empowering Kids and Building Self-Esteem

Most of the parents I speak to would put self-esteem at the top of their list of concerns for their children or teens with learning or attention challenges. And rightly so, as confidence and self-esteem often take a beating when students struggle in school or with homework.

"You're so awesome!"

"You're so smart!"

"You're an amazing athlete!"

Praise is good, right? But what *kind* of praise? Our students with dyslexia, attention deficit, giftedness, and other learning differences are plenty smart, but praising them for being smart may have the opposite effect of what you might expect.

*New York Magazine* published an article by Po Bronson called "How Not to Talk to Your Kids: The Inverse Power of Praise." In it, he discusses a study of 400 fifth graders in New York schools by Carol Dweck[7] and her team at Columbia University. Their findings indicate that praising kids for being smart actually caused them to give up more easily and back off from trying things that might be challenging–better to give up or choose an easier task than to not live up to being smart.

Some of our very bright students who struggle with reading or some aspect of learning, absolutely shut down when praised. They don't believe it and feel they can't live up to it. However, there are ways to give students the encouragement that they need to keep going and develop confidence in themselves as learners.

Here are some tips for empowering our kids.

### *Praise efforts, not smarts:*

"You kept at this problem even though it was hard! You never gave up!"

"You finished this whole math page without getting distracted once!"

"You were really looking for times when you could make a pass in soccer today!"

### *Celebrate small steps:*

"I noticed you got your homework copied in your planner for two classes! That's a great habit that will help you all through school!"

### *Celebrate the strengths:*

"I like how you always take time to put your homework in your homework folder."

### *Focused praise helps them see strategies:*

"You're getting more independent because you've been taking the time to read the directions on each assignment. Great job!"

### *Mistakes are tools by which we learn:*

"Every time we make a mistake, it gives our brain a chance to learn! The brain is like a muscle. When it has to work hard to solve a problem or think about something hard, it grows stronger, just like a muscle!"

## Is Retention Ever a Good Idea?

As spring approaches each year, some parents will get the news that their child is "in danger of retention," meaning their child might have to repeat the grade they are in.

"In danger" indicates that retention is a bad thing. While it is something that should certainly be decided with careful thought, there are times when retention is actually a good idea.

Children grow and develop at different rates, especially in the early years. It is not unusual for a child, particularly a boy, to be developmentally young for his chronological age. Developmental age is not about achievement or intelligence, but rather the child's overall maturity level–the age at which he is functioning as a total organism–socially, emotionally, intellectually, and physically.

Children who are chronologically young for their grade–those whose birthdate is within three months of the cut-off date for entering kindergarten–tend to be at a disadvantage as they go through school. They're always just a little behind the rest in truly being ready for the expectations of the grade level. Many perform in school just fine, but there is often a cost in increased stress, dependence, or time. They have to work harder to manage the demands. There is a true advantage to being one of the older kids in the class.

### When should a child be retained in a grade?

The only solution to being young is time. If your child is struggling in school because he is chronologically or developmentally young, he needs the gift of time. Another year in preschool, kindergarten, or even first grade will give him the time he needs to mature and be ready for the attention and learning demands of the grade level. This is a gift that given once, will support him throughout his school career.

### What are the risks of retention to consider?

The older a child gets, the harder it is to retain them, even if you know they would benefit. Young children believe what their parents say and will usually be fine with whatever is decided, but by second or third grade, the child and his peers may begin to look at retention as a failure. This adds a whole new layer of challenge. The whole family, including the child, need to be on board with retention at this age, and success with it may require a change in schools.

### What will my child say to friends?

Both of my children had fall birthdates and were a bit young for their age. This is a double whammy–being both chronologically and developmentally young–so we kept them in preschool an extra year before starting kindergarten. This meant they were always among the oldest in their class.

When classmates started to ask, "Why are you six and I'm only five?" we told our kids to say, "My parents thought I was too young to start kindergarten last year." They got to blame it on us, and it gave them something to say. Whether their peers understood the explanation or not didn't matter because they really didn't care that much. Sometimes, we just have to give our kids something to say.

## Signs that your child might be chronologically or developmentally young for his grade:

- Gravitates to younger playmates
- Excessively tired after school
- Still taking naps when other children have outgrown them
- Always gets a slow start in the new school year and starts to catch up in the second semester
- Not showing learning disabilities, but always seems to need more help or time
- Whiny about school
- Less coordinated than their peers
- Writing seems larger and less mature than their classmates'

## Will retention solve a learning challenge?

This question gets a resounding no! Immaturity or lack of school attendance for an extended period of time are really the only reasons to retain. Learning and attention challenges, learning disabilities, and dyslexia will *not* go away with time.

These challenges are nearly always the result of weak underlying learning/processing skills. The only way to effectively and permanently change learning challenges is to identify the weak underlying skills and develop them through targeted and intensive cognitive training. Once the brain is receiving clear, complete, and accurate information to think with, the reading, math, and other academic skills can be remediated and caught up.

Most students with learning or attention challenges can and should become comfortable, independent learners at grade level. Retention is probably not the answer for these students, and school and traditional tutoring will probably not solve the problem, but the needed underlying learning and academic skills *can* be developed.

## Food for Thought: Help Your Child Eat for Success

*New Year's resolutions:*

1. Eat healthy

2. Exercise

3. Be awesome!

Yep! We all do it! Every January, adults the world over make resolutions to eat better, get more exercise, and appreciate themselves and others more. We seem to inherently know that these things are important to our health. Did you know these things are exactly what kids need too?

What is frequently overlooked is the tremendous impact that diet, movement, and feelings of appreciation have on attention and learning. As a parent or teacher, it isn't too late to think about adding these things to your students' daily routine. Some small changes today could bring about major changes in your students' lives.

### *Food for thought*

Studies have shown that what we eat affects how we feel, how we think, and how much energy we have. Memory, thinking, and attention are strongly influenced by food.

Believe it or not, the most important nutrient for the brain is fat because the brain is actually made up of fat. The problem is, if we eat a lot of unhealthy fats, we end up with an unhealthy brain.

Fats that support brain health are monounsaturated fats (found in foods like olive oil, canola oil, nuts, and avocados) and some forms of polyunsaturated fats, including omega-3 essential fatty acids, which are particularly important for brain function. Omega-3 fatty acids can be found in cold-water fatty fish, deep-green leafy vegetables, some grains, and pumpkin seeds. Many people find it helpful to supplement their intake of these essential omega-3s by taking fish oil capsules.

The fats to stay away from are saturated fats and trans-fatty acids. Saturated fats are found in meat and full-fat dairy products. We need protein in our diet, much of which comes from these sources, but limiting the amount of saturated fat to about 10 percent of our daily caloric intake is wise, as saturated fat makes the brain cells sluggish. According to Dr. David Perlmutter,[8] author of *The Better Brain Book*, a diet high in saturated fats can result in memory problems and mood disorders for individuals of any age. It is not just seniors who are having "senior moments" these days. Trans-fatty acids are probably the worst fats for our brains and should be on our diet black list. These are found in nearly all processed foods (partially hydrogenated vegetable oil or partially hydrogenated vegetable shortening) and fried foods.

Trans-fatty acids are used to increase the shelf life of food, but inhibit our learning and performance because they make our brain cells rigid, tough, and slow. They keep cells from being able to get nutrients, make energy, and communicate with other cells.

Carbohydrates are important foods for providing energy for the body. But just as with fats, there are good and bad choices. Sugar and white flour are two of the worst. They are simple carbohydrates, so they enter the bloodstream very quickly. They rapidly raise blood sugar levels, which is associated with memory problems. Sugar robs our bodies of B vitamins and nutrients needed to support a stable nervous system and blood sugar balance, affecting health, moods, attention, memory, and behavior. Be aware that there is an extremely high sugar content in juice (eating the whole fruit is better) and that our bodies react to artificial sweeteners other than stevia in the same way as sugar.

Maintaining consistent blood sugar levels allows the brain to get the steady flow of sugar (glucose) needed to keep it fit and functioning. Spikes and fluctuations in blood sugar cause sugar overload, which can cause an individual to have very high, sometimes excessive energy, followed by low energy, sleepiness, or moodiness. Over time, chronic sugar overload can lead to serious illnesses. William Duffy, in his article, "Refined Sugar: The Sweetest Poison of All" says, "Excessive sugar has a strong mal-effect on the functioning of the brain. Too much sugar makes one sleepy; our ability to calculate and remember is lost." This is definitely not a good prescription for learning!

Since we do need carbohydrates for energy and to help protein (in the form of tryptophan) enter the brain cells, complex carbohydrates will be the better choices. These digest more slowly, enter the bloodstream more gradually, and create a gentler rise in blood sugar. Whole grains, fruits, legumes, and vegetables are complex carbohydrates.

Protein is extremely important to our brain function and learning. It helps increase serotonin in the brain, which improves feelings of well-being, hopefulness, organization, and concentration.

Many children go to school after having a sugary carbohydrate breakfast, and many teens choose to go to school with no breakfast at all. A low-sugar breakfast and lunch with 12–20 grams of protein can make a vast difference in a learner's performance.

## Sleep Improves Memory, Learning, and Emotional Regulation

Everybody sleeps, so we don't always stop to consider just how important it is to mental and physical health and academic and social success. Sleep is a complex function that affects almost every type of tissue and system in the body, including the brain, heart, lungs, metabolism, mood, and immune system.

Sleep is the time when learning that happens during the day gets processed and set into memory. It also appears to play a key role in regulating emotion.[9] Emotions that we experience during waking hours are reviewed and processed in a safe, non-reactive way during REM sleep when our muscles are paralyzed so that we can be observers, but cannot physically participate or act out the emotions.

The American Academy of Pediatrics recommends that children ages six to twelve get at least nine hours of sleep. Teens need eight to ten hours, and adults need seven to nine.

Here are some things you can do to help yourself and your family get the sleep they need:

- Create a bedtime routine, starting with cutting off screen time one hour before bedtime. The blue light produced by devices reduces melatonin production, the natural chemical that causes us to get sleepy. In addition, screen time right before bed stimulates the brain and signals the body to stay awake when it should be winding down.

- Set a schedule–go to bed and wake up at the same time each day.
- You want to get a consistent amount of sleep each night. If you or your kids, especially your teens, find that your sleep cycle is off–you're falling asleep too late and having trouble getting up in the morning–try stepping outside for a minute or two as close to waking as possible. Do the same around sunset. Taking in sunlight at these times of day when the sun is low in the sky will gradually reset your internal clock for waking and sleeping. It only takes a few minutes, but be sure to actually step outside. Studies indicate that being outside in sunlight is fifty times quicker and more effective than looking out a window.[10]
- Avoid caffeine or exercise within a few hours of bedtime because they're also stimulating.
- Keep the temperature below seventy degrees. The body heating up can cause wakefulness.

### Don't Tell Me to Try Harder

Be careful about using the words "try harder." In spite of what it may look like, I find that our struggling students are often trying much harder and putting out far more effort than their peers, but unfortunately, trying harder doesn't always work for them, and being told to try harder can shut them off.

Believe it or not, trying too hard can be counter-productive. In order to be an efficient learner of anything, we need to be able to use all of our mental resources. Our two hemispheres in the brain each have unique thinking capabilities which complement each other and work best in cooperation. The right side of the brain lets us experience the whole or the big picture. It is more intuitive and less structured.

The left side is logical, orderly, and verbal. It allows us to break information into small bits in order to learn new things and communicate. When both hemispheres of the brain work together, learning can be easier and more fun. Telling a struggling learner to try harder may actually cause him to overfocus with the left side of the brain. He will try and try to make sense of the pieces, but without the big-picture support of the right brain, he will become more confused and frustrated. Dr. Paul Dennison of the Educational Kinesiology Foundation calls this "switching off."

The cycle of being stuck can often be broken by movement. Integrating movements for this purpose can be found in Brain Gym activities (www.braingym.org). Our words can also help trigger clearer thinking for learning. Instead of saying, "Try harder," try saying something like, "You got this part exactly right. Now let's take a look at this part."

### Respect the effort

Being smart but having to work harder and longer than anyone else in your class, or trying hard and failing anyway is painful for both the individuals with the learning challenges and their families. As we work with our children or our students with learning difficulties, we first need to respect the great amount of extra effort that is needed for them to perform. Constantly reinforcing that effort and celebrating each small success encourages them to keep going.

### Ask for More of the Good Stuff

When my friend Eva read her daughter's first college writing class paper, she was more than a little surprised to see an A at the top. The writing actually wasn't very good, but the teacher had circled things throughout the paper in red and written comments such as, "Give me more of this" or "Good description here."

Eva's daughter got an A on every paper she wrote for the class, and the teacher continued to comment on what she liked and wanted more of. At the end of the semester, Eva's daughter complained, "I didn't learn a thing in that class!" But Eva was extremely impressed with her daughter's final paper. She had learned so much!

Students who struggle academically make lots of mistakes. Being in constant need of correction can be discouraging and defeating. As a parent or teacher, try focusing less on correcting and ask for more of the good stuff! Focus on what you want more of!

### *Validate <u>and</u> move on*

A very effective way to work with discouraged, shutdown learners, or anyone, really, is to validate something about their performance and move on. For example, "The numbers in this problem are lined up perfectly. Can you line up the numbers in the next problem just like that?"

Notice we didn't say, "The numbers in this problem are lined up perfectly, but you need to fix the numbers in the next problem." The word *but* negates everything that came before it.

If a student is slow to get started on his assignment but he's gotten his name on the paper, validate that. "You got your name on the paper; that's always the first step in getting started. Now let's take a look at the first question."

This feels completely different than, "You've had twenty minutes and you've only gotten your name on your paper. You should have had this done by now."

We all need approval, particularly boys, so validate and move on. With consistency, this will increase both attitude and productivity.

## 3 Simple Ways to Control Stress and Screen Fatigue

The year 2020 brought a whole new take on online learning. Students went from doing research online or perhaps taking one or two online classes to spending hours and hours every day doing distance learning on their devices. Adults and children began to experience extreme screen fatigue.

Learning in an online environment requires a different kind of focus than learning in a three-dimensional classroom. In the classroom, there is opportunity for the eyes to move, vary the focal distance, and use peripheral as well as central vision. Watching a screen for long periods of time places a stressful demand on the fine motor muscles around the eyes to stay tightly focused. This focal vision activates our sympathetic nervous system, which stimulates the body's fight or flight response, making you feel agitated and like you want to move.

Since extensive screen time has become inherent in most people's daily lives, here are three simple ways to destress your system and reduce screen fatigue.

### 20/20/20

Every twenty minutes, look twenty feet away for twenty seconds. This gives your eye muscles a chance to relax briefly every twenty minutes, reducing stress and increasing your capacity for mental focus.

### Peripheral vision

Look up from your screen and consciously notice what's in your peripheral vision. You will feel an immediate settling and reduction in stress. Our eyes provide us one of the very few ways we can consciously access and regulate our sympathetic nervous system.

### Step outside!

Looking into the open down-regulates the nervous system immediately. The targeted vision needed to focus on a screen increases arousal or stress. Neuroscience studies at Stanford University indicate that when you step outside and look at the horizon or a wide view, you don't look at any one thing for very long. By keeping your head still, you can expand your gaze to see far above, below, and to the sides of you. This panoramic vision activates the brain stem to reduce the vigilance and arousal of the fight-or-flight stress response.[11]

These three visual hacks allow us to immediately reduce stress by changing the way we view our environment. They are simple, quick, and free! Because of neuroplasticity, the brain's ability to rewire and develop new connections and pathways, the more we practice these simple techniques, the more quickly and easily we can access a calmer, more focused state.

# TAKE THE STONE OUT OF THE SHOE

[7] Carol Dweck is the author of *Mindset, The New Psychology of Success*. This is a work on motivation and growth mindset, a concept we have found to be powerful in helping students succeed.

[8] Perlmutter, David, MD *The Better Brain Book*. New York, NY: Riverhead Books, 2004.

[9] Huberman, Andrew. Huberman Lab Podcast Episode 5, "Why We Dream," Feb. 1, 2021.

Vandekerckhove, Marie and Wang, Yu-Lin "Emotion, emotion regulation and sleep: An intimate relationship," AIMS Neuroscience.

[10] Huberman, Andrew. Huberman Lab Podcast Episode 2, "Master Your Sleep and Be More Alert When Awake," Jan. 11, 2021.

[11] Wapner, Jessica. "Vision and Breathing May Be the Secrets to Surviving 2020," Scientific American, Nov. 2020.

Huberman, Andrew. Huberman Lab Podcast Episode 10, "Master Stress: Tools for Managing Stress and Anxiety," March 7, 2021.

JILL STOWELL

Chapter Ten
# ATTENTION AND FOCUS

## Child's Play Develops Attention

"Look how high I can climb!"

"Watch me do a handstand!"

"Look at me jump!"

Young children love to show off their physical prowess. What parents may not realize is that the antics kids use to get attention are often building blocks for developing attention!

All the running, jumping, climbing, doing handstands, and rolling down hills that kids love to do when they have the time and space to do it plays a tremendously important role in the development of self-control and attention.

Believe it or not, free, unstructured, physical playtime is a big contributor to school success. In his book *A User's Guide to the Brain*, John Ratey, MD says, "Mounting evidence shows that movement is crucial to every other brain function, including memory, emotion, language, and learning. Our 'higher' brain functions have evolved from movement and still depend on it."

Learning begins with movement. Babies begin to learn about themselves and their environment through movement. Visual skills are developed through movement. Understanding of left and right and a sense of balance and control is developed first through movement. Movement helps energize and organize the brain.

Physical balance is the foundation for attention and mental control. The body must be relaxed and centered to truly be balanced, and we learn about balance through movement.

The wild abandon kids seem to be born with is there for a reason. Encourage it and give lots of opportunities for "child's play!"

## Balance, the Foundation of Attention Training

When we do **Attention Focus Training** at Stowell Learning Centers, we start with physical activities such as walking slowly forward and backward on a line or low balance beam that requires the student to be balanced and centered. Going slowly and maintaining control can be very difficult for students at first. At each step of increasing control, we have students stop and recognize or *feel* the change from distracted, speedy, and off-balance to calm and focused.

We work with students on anchoring the calm, focused feeling by taking a slow, deep breath and thinking about an X, an integrated symbol that engages both hemispheres of the brain. Then, when they start to get distracted and unfocused while doing school-type activities and homework, they can take a deep breath, think about the X, and remember what it felt like to be balanced and in control. This helps them access that feeling of calm, centered focus so they can bring more attention to the task.

# TAKE THE STONE OUT OF THE SHOE

## *Applications for parents:*

- Less screen time and more unstructured outdoor time is important, especially for young children.
- Activities that require balance, such as gymnastics and martial arts, can help improve attention focus.
- Short movement breaks during homework are time well spent.
- Try having kids balance on two feet, one foot, while walking on a line or curb forward and backward, or maybe even doing handstands for a few minutes when distracted. As they fight for balance, they are also fighting for attention and learning to center their body and mind.

## 5 Steps to Developing Impulse Control

*Dear Teacher,*
*Why did I do it?*
*I don't know.*
*—Your Student*

Braden leans forward in his chair and snips off Norah's braid. Why? It was there, and he wondered what it would look like falling off.

Educationandbehavior.com

Toby stands up and walks around the classroom humming and beat-boxing. Why?

He doesn't know. In fact, he seems completely unaware he's doing it.

Tori wants to swing, so she pushes Mari off.

Impulsivity or action without thought is often a characteristic of children with ADHD. It can lead to behaviors and consequences that baffle and frustrate parents, teachers, and classmates. It isolates kids and affects their self-esteem and friendships.

At a neutral time, not in the midst of bad or impulsive behavior, work through these steps to help your child develop impulse control. Take the time to really explore and practice. Monitor and check in frequently to reinforce the new idea until it becomes a habit.

### Step 1: Awareness

The first step in making any change is awareness. Explore the word *impulsive*. What does it mean? What does it look like when someone is impulsive? What would it look like if that person stopped to think before acting?

### Step 2: What they do

Help children think specifically about what they do when they are being impulsive. What does it look like? Do they interrupt others? Do they grab things? Do they move too fast? This is an important step because they have to begin to recognize their own behavior.

### Step 3: Another way

Dialogue specific situations where the child (including teens) tends to be impulsive. How does the impulsive behavior affect others? How does it affect the child? How could the child respond differently? Then what would the outcome look like? Visualize or role play and dialogue this.

### Step 4  Count backward

As soon as the student recognizes the beginnings of his impulsive thought or action, he should count backward: "Five, four, three, two, one." This interrupts the impulsive pattern long enough for him to ask, "Who's in control?" and make another choice.

### Step 5  Who's in control?

We all want to be the boss of ourselves. Help children understand that when they are impulsive, they are not really in control. With young students, we call their impulsiveness "Mr. Impulsive."

After counting backward from five to one, teach the student to say, "Who is in control?" or "Is Mr. Impulsive in control, or am I in control?"

Then, teach them to take a deep breath, think, and make a different choice.

These steps will need to be discussed and practiced over and over in real time in order to create a new awareness and pattern of behavior, but be patient! The month or so that you have to intentionally, frequently, and consistently practice with your child may save you both years of frustration.

## The Brain on ADHD–Flowcharts to the Rescue

Individuals with ADHD often chatter nonstop, flit from topic to topic, and have trouble completing tasks. Their busy brains have so much to think about all at one time!

### Good at academics, poor at follow-through

Jennifer can think about several different things at one time. She can read out loud and be thinking of something completely different. She finds that she can follow a conversation and think about several other things at the same time.

Her attention switches from one topic to another instantaneously, and often right in the middle of a task, conversation, or test item.

Jennifer has some very good academic skills, especially in reading, but her weak ability to focus her mind on one thing for any amount of time makes it difficult to evaluate, apply, or work in steps with the information she learns. Most of the assignments she has in school feel like they require too much time because it is so hard for her to maintain her attention on anything of length and to focus on details and sequential steps.

### Go with your strength

Lack of follow-through can make having an ADHD group member frustrating, but these are exactly the kids we want leading the brainstorming sessions and contributing ideas for creative ways to present material and solve problems.

### Flowcharts build independent follow through

We have found flowcharts to be a very helpful tool for our disorganized kids who struggle with following steps and task completion.

A flowchart is a visual way to take a big idea, project, decision, assignment, or problem and break it down into small, sequential steps. It helps students understand what needs to be done, get started, and keep going. It helps them move forward with a feeling of confidence instead of feeling overwhelmed.

Building flowcharts together helps students think about all the pieces of an assignment or task. It provides an opportunity to explore how much time is needed and to dialogue a logical sequence for completion.

Students can check off each step as they go, which allows them to self-monitor their progress and feel successful every step of the way.

**The steps**

A simple flowchart is made up of three main types of symbols:

- Ovals, which signify the start or end of a process;

- Rectangles, which show instructions or actions; and

- Diamonds, which show decisions that must be made or questions to be asked.

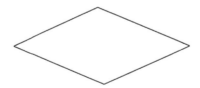

- Symbols are connected one to the other by arrows to show the flow of the process.

Here is a sample flowchart. Notice every little step is included. Following the arrows gives students direction every step of the way, allowing them to be more independent and feel success as they complete each step.

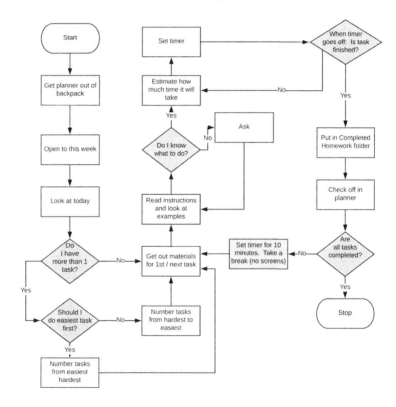

### *Saved!*

Justin's parents just shook their heads in disbelief day after day as their extremely bright, attention-challenged son sat surrounded by his homework papers and books and did nothing!

Justin had good intentions, but he was so disorganized that he simply could not get started. And once he was stuck, his creative mind took him on all kinds of fascinating journeys. Needless to say, Justin was failing every subject in the seventh grade.

Together with Justin, we built a flowchart with every single step needed to get homework tasks ordered, completed, and put in appropriate folders, including short breaks. Having the visual to follow allowed Justin to know exactly how to get started, keep track of what to do next, and feel successful every step of the way. Within two weeks, he was independently completing his homework. What a huge boost for his self-esteem!

Remember, do not create the flowchart *for* your child. Do it together. By dialoguing, visualizing, and sequencing each step together, you are giving your child practice with critical executive function skills. Guide your student in creating the flowchart. This will allow her to see exactly how it works and build buy-in and ownership.

### Simple Focus Strategies

Having to constantly get your child back on task is frustrating for everyone involved. Here are some simple focus strategies that you can try.

### Timer

Use a timer for children or teens who have trouble sticking with a task. Start wherever they are, even if it's only five minutes, and gradually increase the amount of time. When the timer goes off, celebrate; then reset for the next five minutes. This helps your child build his ability to focus and keeps you accountable to check in regularly.

The use of the timer is not to time them, get them to work faster, or get a certain amount done before the time goes off. The goal with the timer is for students to really focus on the task for that finite, manageable amount of time. This builds their understanding of what it feels like to really tune in and be in control of their focus. The tiny little celebration breaks give them a chance to feel good about their accomplishment and mentally regroup.

### Movement Minute

Recognize the limits of your student's ability to concentrate before becoming unproductive. Take a "Movement Minute" to re-energize thinking and focus. Bounce on an exercise ball, stand and take a good stretch, wrestle with the dog for a minute, have a one-minute dance party, or get up and get a drink of water. Keep it short, include movement, and don't include screens or devices!

### Thought Box

Some children just have to tell you what they are thinking the second it pops into their minds. They may be in the middle of a math assignment or a science lesson, but now they're telling you about a video game they like. Even though you try to redirect, they just can't help themselves, and the off-task words keep coming.

# TAKE THE STONE OUT OF THE SHOE

We don't want kids to think that what they have to say is not valuable, but they do have to learn to inhibit and stay on task or on topic. The "Thought Box" is a fun, easy tool that helps students recognize their drifting thoughts and set them aside to share or explore at a later time.

Have the student visualize a special box where he will put his thoughts/ideas/things he wants to say when it is not the right time to share them. This validates that what he is thinking is valuable and isn't being thrown away or forgotten, but that this is not what he needs to be focusing on right now.

Practice using the thought box and then devise a cue between the parent or teacher and student that will be used to help the student begin using the thought box during school or homework time. Specify a time during the day (and eventually perhaps just once a week) when the student can share something out of his thought box.

### Getting Started Questions

Together with the student, make a list of the first three things that he needs to do to get started. Before starting each assignment, the student should read and use his questions to help him get started immediately and independently.

For example:

- What materials do I need?
- Did I put my name on the paper?
- Where is the first set of instructions?

Chapter Eleven
# EXECUTIVE FUNCTION AND ORGANIZATION

## The Right Amount of Control/Personal CEO

Ed's six-year-old son was being very childish and annoying. "Stop acting like a child!" Dad exclaimed, exasperated. Then he heard what had just come out of his mouth! "Wait! He *is* a child!"

### What parents and teachers want

We want kids to act like kids–their exuberance, laughter, energy, and wonder is a gift to hold onto! But let's add the caveat that they also focus, think, plan, organize, make good decisions, have self-control, and evaluate and learn from their mistakes!

In other words, we want kids to be kids with the benefit of great executive function skills. Hold on! Not so fast! These skills are frontal lobe functions that develop throughout childhood, but the frontal lobe develops last in our brains, so the major growth in executive function occurs in the teens through the mid-twenties.

### Think of executive function like a mental dialogue

If you think about how you make decisions, plan out your week, or tackle a problem or project, you will see that it usually involves a combination of visualizing and talking through things in your mind. Visual and verbal inner language are two key components of working memory and executive function that can be developed in students at school and at home with consistent and intentional instruction throughout the day.

The little bit of extra time it will take to help children and teens improve their inner dialogue and visualization skills has a big payoff in greater retention, comprehension, and independence.

## Are You Building Or *Being* Their Executive Function?

### Great teacher, wrong kind of help

Teachers who give very explicit, detailed instructions of exactly what to do every step of the way on a project or assignment or who tell students exactly how and when and what to study for a test are often viewed as wonderful teachers. Their students thrive with the structure, and everyone feels great, until the next teacher comes along who isn't as detailed and the students don't know how to think for themselves.

### Helicopter parents

Well-meaning "helicopter" parents hover over their struggling learners and guide them every single step of the way. They provide an amazing safety net for their kids. But they may be keeping their kids from exactly what they most want for them—to become independent!

## Building executive function through self-questioning

In their desire to help students be successful, parents and teachers may inadvertently take on the role of the students' executive function.

What students really need is to exercise their own executive function skills so they can think, plan, organize, and manage themselves.

This often just requires a slight shift in our language–moving from *telling* students every single step they need to take, to engaging them in an age-appropriate dialogue that guides them in determining steps and strategies. Here's what this might look like:

*Being* the students' executive function: "You have a book report due in two weeks. You need to pick a book that has eighty pages and read ten pages every day."

*Building* executive function: "You have a book report due in two weeks. Let's create a plan for getting the book read and the report done without stressing out at the last minute." Then engage students' thinking through questions such as:

- What are the things you have to do to complete this project? (Pick a book, read, write.)
- How much time do you need for each part of the project?
- How many pages can you read every day? How long of a book should you choose?

These questions are the kinds of things that we, through our executive function, ask ourselves. As students get more adept at this self-questioning process, you will be able to make your questions broader, so they are engaging more of their own executive function. For example, you might eventually ask, "What questions do you need to ask yourself as you plan out this project?"

## Develop Visualization as a Comprehension and Memory Tool

- Guide students in visualizing each step in a sequence of events, project, science experiment, etcetera. Have them look up (to engage the visual modality) and imagine each step/event on a specific spot on the walls or in the air in front of them. Have them point to and describe the image. Enhance key points in the image by changing the size, adding color or humor, or connecting images in some way.
- Encourage students to visualize their day, planner, or calendar to improve time concepts and management. Have them point to various events in their image.
- Before packing up for the day, have students visualize and verbalize what materials will be needed for their homework.
- Guide students in visualizing and dialoguing exactly what written instructions on assignments are asking
- Teach students to visualize test questions and all answer choices before choosing a response.

## Steps to Helping Children and Teens Develop Executive Function and Problem-Solving Skills

Learning to create and use strategies to monitor and evaluate behavior and attention is literally training executive function. Applying the use of strategies to problem-solving of any kind involves the following:

- Being aware that there is a problem
- Identifying exactly what the problem is
- Brainstorming possible solutions or strategies
- Evaluating how well each strategy will work and what the outcome will be
- Deciding on the best solution/strategy
- Committing to trying it
- Evaluating whether the outcome was what was expected
- Modifying the strategy as needed

These are steps we can use to help children develop executive function and study skills. Through dialoguing, modeling, practicing, and evaluating together, we can help children become more and more capable of managing their own behavior, choices, attention, and studies.

### Applying these steps for Kasey

Remember Kasey? She was the student we met earlier who had so much pent-up energy by the time recess arrived that she bolted out the door, bumping into others and knocking things over. In the following example, we will show how applying these steps might look in Kasey's situation:

- **Being aware that there is a problem:** Kasey's parent or teacher can re-enact the scene with Kasey, helping her notice the things and people she bumps or tramples as she races for the door when the bell rings.

- **Identifying exactly what the problem is:** Kasey has weak auditory processing and language skills, so sitting in a class that requires listening and note-taking is like torture for her. By the time the bell rings, she's ready to jump out of her skin. The problem for Kasey is that she is so uncomfortable by the end of class that she just has to get out of the class and move, *now*!

- **Brainstorming possible solutions or strategies together:**
    - Possible solution #1: Kasey could be released for recess early.

    - Possible solution #2: Kasey could sit right next to the door.

    - Possible solution #3: Kasey could be restricted from going to recess every time she races out the door.

    - Possible solution #4: Kasey could sit closer to the door and be put in charge of opening the door for recess.

- **Visualize and dialogue each strategy to evaluate how well it will work and what the outcome will be.**

#1: Could keep other students from getting knocked around, but it may cause Kasey to miss assignments given at the end of the period and cause other students to be mad at her for going to recess early.

#2: Kasey can get out the door quickly without having to navigate through the rest of the students. This meets Kasey's need to move and the teacher's need to keep other students safe. It does not take any extra time.

#3: This might eventually help Kasey remember not to run out the door but does not meet her need to move.

#4: Giving Kasey the responsibility of opening the door for the class (and teaching the class that they are to wait until the door is opened before heading for the door) gets Kasey to the door first and gives her something important to do that provides a reason to be less impulsive and more intentional about going to the door.

Kasey and her teacher can decide on the best solution (either #2 or #4). Both need to commit to trying it for a given amount of time (one to five days) and then evaluate together how it is working. They should modify the strategy as needed.

If solution #2 is chosen, they might find that Kasey is still impulsively racing out the door, though no one is in her way. To help Kasey be more intentional about controlling her impulsiveness and speed, they might decide to try solution #4, with the caveat that a leader has to be an example. The teacher might (privately) have Kasey role-play/practice several times, saying to herself, "When the bell rings, I walk slowly to the door," and then doing it.

This strategy is worth the time it takes, as it helps students become more independent and responsible and feel better about themselves.

## 7 Easy Organizational Strategies to Help Students Start the School Year Right

People are creatures of habit. If we create structure and habits around homework from the very beginning of the school year, there will be fewer battles and negotiations later.

These may seem obvious to you, but they are not obvious or easy for many students. Each strategy will take instruction, practice, and monitoring in order to become comfortable and routine. Invest the time–it's worth it!

- Determine a set-in-stone **homework time** for each day that will be kept free of appointments, phone calls, texting, etc.
- Set up a specific **homework space** that is well-lit, quiet, free from distractions, clear of clutter and devices, and stocked with all of the materials needed.
- Teach students how to use an **assignment sheet or planner.** Explore how it is organized, how and when to fill it in, and how to use it as a tool at home.
- **Avoid misplaced homework.** Determine *exactly* what should be done with homework when it is completed and practice putting it there for every single assignment.
- **Get homework turned in.** The student should visualize and orally talk through the procedure for turning in his homework in *each* class.
- Carefully review the **class syllabus** and expectations. Put projects, tests, and other important dates in the planner, even if they are weeks or months away.
- Help students notice, carefully **read**, and understand **written instructions** before starting assignments.

# TAKE THE STONE OUT OF THE SHOE

Most students do not love doing homework, so creating routines and structure around homework is beneficial for most families and for students of all ages.

## Getting Homework Put Away and Turned In: A Strategy for Creating New Habits

Students with attention or executive function challenges often experience the frustration of working very hard to complete their homework and then losing it or forgetting to turn it in. Good intentions and reminders from others are not generally enough to solve this problem. The student needs to have a plan for putting homework away and getting it turned in, and it must be practiced and monitored until it becomes a habit.

The strategy below for putting homework away and getting it turned in can be applied to any number of areas where a new habit needs to be created.

### *Strategy*

- The parent or teacher *and* student should determine exactly what should be done with homework when it is completed.
- When the student finishes an assignment, the parent can ask, "What do you need to do with your completed homework?"
- The student should talk through the process *orally*, saying, "I finished my math homework, so I put it in the math section of the binder." Once this is a stable procedure, have him *mentally* talk himself through the process.
- Discuss how homework is collected in *each* class. The student should visualize and orally talk through the process of turning in his homework in each

class, mentally hearing the teacher ask for the homework at the beginning of class, visualizing himself putting the homework in the designated homework box, etc.

For example, the student might verbalize to their parent while visualizing the following:

- I walk into math class. I go to my desk, which is in the third row, and I sit down and put my backpack down next to me on my left side.

- I open my backpack and take out my folder. I go to the math section and take out my math homework. I put the math homework on the right-front corner of my desk.

- When the teacher starts to talk, I look right at her and hear her saying to pass our papers to the person on our left. I see myself picking up my math homework and handing it to Sam, who sits next to me.

Starting with one or two classes, the student should visualize and verbalize turning in his homework in detail just before going to bed at night and before going to school in the morning. This should be done every day until the student is successfully and consistently turning in his homework in the given classes. Then he can begin to visualize and mentally rehearse the process (instead of orally) and can add on more classes when ready.

### Metacognition: The Art of Self-Talk

Metacognition is literally **thinking about thinking**. Parents and teachers can help stimulate metacognition in students by asking questions that cause them to reflect on how they are learning or approaching a task.

By modeling self-talk and intentionally discussing and teaching students to ask themselves questions, parents and teachers can help students become more active thinkers, better comprehenders, and more independent learners.

Many parents express frustration over their student's lack of organization, listening, and following directions. Here are some examples of self-questioning to increase organization:

- Are my materials all together and ready for tomorrow?
- What materials do I need to bring home from school in order to complete my homework? Do I have them?
- In what order can I best complete these assignments?
- How does this paper need to look when it's finished?
- How long will this project/report take? What steps are involved?
- How many pages do I need to read each day in order to finish this book for my test?
- What is my first step in getting started?
- Where am I most focused when doing my homework?
- Where do I put my completed homework?
- When is the test?
- What kind of questions does the teacher usually ask?
- What are my best strategies for studying?

### Examples of self-questioning to increase listening and following directions:

- Am I listening carefully, or is my attention drifting?
- What can I do to tune in better?
- How do I know when the teacher or my parent is giving directions?
- Did I read and understand the directions?
- Are there any keywords in the directions?
- Did I answer every question? Did I complete them all?

Intentionally teaching students how to self-question takes time and monitoring but brings self-control and self-management to a more conscious level and hopefully brings more ownership on the part of the student. Metacognition is how we naturally guide our choices and behaviors, and training in this area can be applied to almost anything. Thinking about thinking is a powerful support to learning, attention, and behavior.

Chapter Twelve
# BEHAVIOR AND SOCIAL SKILLS

## Surviving The Fireworks (And Loud Situations) With Your Sensitive Child

If you have a child who is sensitive to loud noises, you may look forward to Fourth of July fireworks with a mixture of anticipation and trepidation!

Think about yourself being startled by a loud noise. Your brain immediately goes on high alert. Survival mode kicks in until you can determine, what it was, where it came from, and if you are safe.

We get startled or frightened by things that are unexpected and that we don't understand. Children with auditory sensitivity and auditory processing challenges may not be able to quickly identify what they're hearing, where it is, and if they are safe, kicking them into fight or flight–translation: running, hiding, screaming, meltdowns, or terror.

Here are five things you can do to help your child weather and maybe even enjoy the fireworks:

### #1 Prepare

Take away the startle factor by preparing your child over and over throughout the day about the really cool thing that they get to see when it gets dark.

### #2 Understand

Explain to your child how fireworks work. Talk about how the firework gets shot into the sky from a special machine, and once it gets really, really high in the sky, it explodes into sparkles and light. The really loud noise they hear is the explosion. Look at YouTube videos to hear the sound and see what it looks like.

### #3 Practice

Pretend to be shooting off a firework. Show the trajectory, reaching up high. Make an explosion sound and use your hands and fingers to be the light exploding and sparkling.

Have your child mimic your demonstration for you and others. If you have a dog that is frightened by fireworks, have your child share with the dog how fireworks work and tell the dog it doesn't have to be afraid. The more your child practices and dialogues about fireworks, the more she patterns in a new, calmer response to them.

### #4 Settle

If your Fourth of July is going to be a busy, stimulating day with family and friends, take twenty or thirty minutes before dark to sit with your child in a calm, quiet space. Read a story, hum, or talk or sit quietly—in other words, take some time to chill and settle. Let your child sit on your lap with your arms wrapped around him, give him some nice, grounding pressure with a weighted blanket or by stroking his back, arms, or legs firmly.

Note: Prepare your child in advance by telling them you are going to take this settling time together and when, so it's not a surprise.

#### #5 Wear Headphones

Put ear muffs or over-the-ear headphones (preferably noise-canceling) on your child for the duration of the fireworks.

These steps can be applied to any situation that you anticipate will be upsetting to your child because it is unexpected, too loud, or too bright.

### Everyone Needs a Hula-Hoop!
#### Helping children understand social space

Have you ever known someone who repeatedly invaded your personal space? They just stood or sat too close in conversation? There is something really uncomfortable about that, even if the person is someone you know and like.

Often, I speak with parents who express concerns about their child's social skills and ability to make and keep friends. While there are many varied skills that go into being a good friend, one of those skills is an awareness and observance of personal social space.

Talking about social space is a good thing, but it's not very concrete, and a child with these challenges may not really get it. A Hula-Hoop can help make this more visual and concrete.

Step into a Hula-Hoop and pull it up around your waist, with the hoop touching your back and extending out in front of you, creating a space between you and the child. Tell the child, "This is my space. This is how far away from me you need to be when we talk." Put the Hula-Hoop around the child and say, "This is your space. Here's where I need to be when we talk so I don't invade your space."

Make the learning fun. Use the word *invade*, and connect it with your child's favorite villain in order to help them understand the word. Then you can practice having conversations without invading each other's space. Use the Hula-Hoop to check the space until it's understood. Then have the child show you his imaginary Hula-Hoop by making an arc with his hands in front of him.

Practice noticing and respecting personal space with family members and close friends. Then talk about noticing personal space in other places and relationships, by imagining the Hula-Hoop.

This same idea can be used to help children who tend to grab materials and things that belong to others. Use the Hula-Hoop to reinforce the understanding that you don't get to touch or grab things in someone else's personal space.

## What Every Parent Wants!
### Building your child's confidence and self-esteem

In a YouTube video, Jessica, a little girl of about five, stands in front of the bathroom mirror and exuberantly says all of the things she likes: "Now, my whole house is great. I can do anything good. I like my school. I like anything. I like my dad. I like my cousins . . ."

What could be better than our children having great self-esteem? Confidence is one of the very top goals that virtually every parent I speak to has for their child or teen.

Struggles in school chip away at a student's self-esteem. No matter how talented they may be in other areas, when smart kids struggle with reading, math, comprehension, or other aspects of school, they know. They know that they take longer than their peers to complete the work. They're the ones who have to stay in at recess or don't have any free time after school because it takes them so long to get through their homework.

They're the ones who study like maniacs with their parents and get an embarrassing test score anyway. They're the ones who are putting so much energy into trying to listen, pay attention, actually read the words on the page, or understand what they're reading or hearing, that they miss instruction or important information.

Students who struggle with learning or attention repeatedly hear the following:

- "Pay attention."
- "You need to try harder."
- "If you were more motivated, you could do this."
- "Just buckle down and do it!"
- "You'll have to redo these."

They (and their parents) may be spending far more time and expending far more effort than their peers but getting a lesser result. This is frustrating and confusing for all.

And kids begin to call themselves dumb. They feed their brains negative self-talk:

- " My teacher hates me."
- "I'll never be able to do this."
- I'm not good at math."
- "I can't read."
- "I hate school."

Follow Jessica's example. Get kids in the habit of daily affirmations. Teach them to say positive things about themselves. The brain loves this! Our words really do matter, even words to ourselves, and can affect how we feel.

## Harness the Power of Words to Improve Learning and Self-Esteem

Every decision we make and everything we do is driven by our beliefs and emotions. Research shows us that there is physiological communication between the heart and the brain and that the thinking part of the brain is highly affected by the emotional part.[12] We also know that our words are very powerful.

Feeling valued and in control will dramatically impact a person's learning. Give specific comments to students about what you observe, like, and appreciate about them.

Have students tell or write what they appreciate about themselves. True feelings of appreciation actually create chemical changes in the brain that empower us to have more clarity and calmness, a good combination for learning and good health!

Always keep in mind how powerful words are. Negative words and comments can also trigger chemical changes in the brain that can stay with a student for many hours, disrupting learning and upsetting self-esteem.

Validate students' efforts and achievements during as well as after completing the task. Break tasks down into smaller, more easily achievable units as needed so students can feel successful often.

Help students to see how far they have come by remembering where they began. This helps them to see and value their accomplishment.

Remember that a little success goes a long way. Pushing a resistant student in a negative way will likely get more resistance. But sincerely celebrating even the smallest success can make that same child sit taller and encourage him to try again.

## Calming Back-to-School Jitters

*"I have a love–hate relationship with the start of school."*
–Parent of a Struggling Student

Sophie did great all summer in her sessions at the learning center. Her confidence was soaring along with her skills. Then, two weeks before the start of school, Sophie started to get stomachaches and nausea. She couldn't sleep and started to get extremely irritable at home.

Sophie was terrified of starting fifth grade. Like many students with learning or attention challenges, memories of last year's struggles flooded her with anxiety.

"What if my teacher doesn't like me?"

"What if I can't do the work?"

"What if everyone thinks I'm dumb?"

"What if I don't understand what to do?"

When students can't process information quickly and easily, it may cause them to feel insecure and anxious in any new situation, and that fear and anxiety pull them out of learning mode and into survival mode–fight or flight.

Some of our students with learning or attention challenges have poor regulation or self-control, so their back-to-school jitters may be over-excitement. They get to see their friends; they're excited to be in the next grade; they can't wait to meet their new teacher. All this exciting stuff may put them over the top and make it almost impossible for them to sit still, stop talking, and pay attention.

How do we get these over-anxious or overly excited kids off to a good start in school?

### 3 Simple strategies for getting the "nail-biters" off to a good start

1. Use a *kinesthetic voice*. The research of Dr. Stephen Porges[13] tells us that a quiet, melodic voice calms the nervous system. Trying to rationalize and think through situations and solutions with a child in a highly anxious state won't work. Try just speaking quietly and gently (about anything) and letting the sound of your voice settle them.

2. Teach students a deep-breathing strategy. Have them inhale and exhale to a mental count of five (breathe in for five and out for five). Breathe in and out through the nose to calm the nervous system. Breathe in through the nose and out through the mouth to release tension.

3. Most teachers supply an information sheet or syllabus at the beginning of the year. Read through, highlight, and discuss classroom rules, expectations, and important dates together. Guide your student in putting the dates on his planner or calendar. This is time well spent, as it helps you and your child know what to expect and gets important time-sensitive information recorded and on your radar.

¹² The Heartmath organization (heartmath.com) has done extensive scientific research over the last twenty-five years, looking at the psychophysiology of stress, emotions, and the interactions between the heart and brain. Over three hundred peer-reviewed or independent studies have been published showing the benefits of the Heartmath techniques and technologies. The Heart Breathing, Em-Wave, and Inner Balance techniques/tools have been very successful with students at Stowell Learning Centers in increasing self-awareness and controlling their own response to stress.

¹³ Stephen Porges, PhD, is the author of The Polyvagal Theory: Neurophysiological Foundations of Emotions, Attachment, Communication, and Self-regulation (Norton, 2011), The Pocket Guide to the Polyvagal Theory: The Transformative Power of Feeling Safe, (Norton, 2017) and co-editor of Clinical Applications of the Polyvagal Theory: The Emergence of Polyvagal-Informed Therapies (Norton, 2018). He is the creator of a music-based intervention, the Safe and Sound Protocol™. Porges's work has brought new understanding to autonomic physiology and reducing the stress response in children and adults in order to increase engagement and ease.

# JILL STOWELL

Chapter Thirteen
# DYSLEXIA, READING, AND SPELLING

## Accommodations and Modifications to Support Dyslexic Students at School and with Homework

Below you will find a list of accommodations that parents and teachers can use to support dyslexic students or other struggling readers in school and in homework. But first, a word of caution:

Accommodations and modifications can be a great support to students who struggle in school. We should give students all the support we can, but it's also important to understand that accommodations and modifications are not a permanent solution. They should be a temporary support while the *real* problem is being corrected.

### Content-area reading, assignments, and worksheets

Dyslexic students can often listen and comprehend well. If appropriate, in subjects like social studies and science, they should be expected to participate in discussions and do all homework assignments with the help of a parent or tutor.

If the assignment is to read a chapter, have the student start reading each section, and then the parent can take over the reading when the student gets tired. Even if the student only reads a sentence, the expectation will be that he can read the text and will start reading after each subheading. Knowing that he can stop when he's tired reduces the pressure. As his reading improves, he will gradually tackle more reading on his own.

When the student comes to a word she doesn't know, she should try to work through the sounds as best she can, not just guess; then the parent can tell her the word as needed.

If an assignment is taking far too long to complete, parents should be allowed to note the amount of time spent and sign off on it. If this happens regularly, the teacher may want to note for the parents which parts of the assignment would be the most important to focus on.

On worksheets, the student should be expected to write the answers to a portion of the questions (for example, two out of five), and an aide or parent can write the answers to the other questions as the student dictates. Again, it is important that the student be responsible for the assignment and have responsibility for part of the writing so he knows he is capable. He should know that the amount of writing he has to do is being reduced so he can focus on neatness and spelling. His best is expected.

### *Content-area tests*

The student should be allowed to take content area tests orally (questions read to her and responses given orally). This way her reading and writing difficulties are not getting in the way of her showing what she knows about the subject.

## Vocabulary

If the student is working on vocabulary definitions, a picture or a few brief words that show he understands the meaning would be much more valuable than copying a textbook or dictionary definition.

## Reading

When reading, the student will likely do best with fairly large print that is not too dense on the page. Dyslexic students may have just as much difficulty with a first-grade-level book as a higher-level book, because the lower the level, the greater the number of trigger words (small, non-conceptual sight words that trigger disorientation). High interest, knowledge of the subject, and more meaningful context will help the dyslexic reader use his good comprehension skills to support his reading.

When the student misreads a word while doing oral reading at an appropriate grade level, have him spell the missed word orally and then attempt to read it again. This will help him notice all of the letters and the order of the letters in the word.

## Assignment sheet/planner

The student needs to learn how to use an assignment sheet. Since copying from the board will be very difficult for him due to his spelling challenges, expect him to copy as much as he can in the time allotted, but at least the first assignment. Gradually increase the amount expected as his skills increase. Also, provide a filled-out assignment sheet for him as long as he has copied down at least one assignment. He has to know that things are expected of him and that he is a capable person, but at the same time needs to be supported while his dyslexia is being remediated.

### Frustration and shutdown

When frustrated or shut down, the student can be cued to take a deep breath to help her refocus. It may be appropriate to have her get up and move (get a drink, sharpen a pencil, do something quick and physical) and then resume the task. This will help her get unstuck.

A great brain break for our dyslexic readers or struggling students of any age is *cross crawls*. Have the student stand and cross one elbow to the opposite knee. Then repeat with the other elbow. Do this, alternating back and forth, for thirty to sixty seconds. This helps students to re-integrate–get both hemispheres of the brain working together for better focus and easier learning.

### Notetaking

Provide the student with a copy of class notes from the teacher or another student the teacher assigns. The student should still take his own notes, but having a complete and accurate set of notes as well will facilitate his studying and understanding.

### Written report alternatives

Offer the student alternative ways to present what she knows. For example, instead of a lengthy written report, allow the student to do an oral presentation or a creative presentation that better fits her thinking style and still allows her to show knowledge of the content.

### Forewarn dyslexic learners when they are expected to read aloud in class

Reading orally in front of peers is unnerving for most people, whether they have challenges or not. If students are expected to read aloud in class, try alerting your struggling

# TAKE THE STONE OUT OF THE SHOE

readers a day in advance that you will be calling on them to read a given paragraph or section so they can rehearse ahead of time.

## *Recorded books increase independence and comprehension*

Having textbooks on audio allows students to spend less time struggling with homework and more time understanding and absorbing the material.

Here are two resources available to schools and parents for a nominal yearly fee (may be free to schools) that will allow students with dyslexia and learning disabilities to access their textbooks on audio:

Learning Ally: www.learningally.org

Bookshare: www.bookshare.org

To get the most out of audiobooks, students should read along in their textbook as they listen. Using their finger under the line of text may help them keep their place and allows them to touch, see, and hear the words simultaneously. This helps students notice vocabulary, see how words look while accurately hearing them read, and increases attention and comprehension.

Research reported by Learning Ally[14] states that students show the following improvement with the use of audiobooks:

- Improved reading comprehension: 76 percent
- Increased interest in reading: 76 percent
- Improved reading accuracy: 52 percent

- Increased self-confidence: 61 percent
- Increased motivation: 67 percent

These are accommodations that may make school and homework more successful and comfortable for dyslexic learners but should not be mistaken for the remediation they also need.

## Increase Decoding Fluency and Visual Attention for Reading

### *Decoding: vowel sound to whole word*

Struggling readers often get stuck in sound-by-sound decoding (saying each sound in the word and then blending them together). This causes their reading to be slow and choppy, and they often forget what sounds they said and end up reading the word incorrectly.

Vowel sounds are like the glue that holds the letters together to make a word. Instead of having the student say each sound and then blend, try having him say the vowel sound and then read the whole word. This helps students focus on that all-important vowel sound and become quicker and more automatic with decoding.

### *Spell-Read*[15]

Purpose:

- Improves left-to-right eye movement
- Trains the brain to notice all of the letters in words
- Improves word reading accuracy
- Reduces impulsivity

Procedure:

- The student spells each word and then reads it.
- The parent or teacher says the word if the student doesn't immediately know it after spelling it.

Do this exercise for five minutes daily before doing regular oral reading. When the student is doing oral reading, have him spell-read words that he can't decode or that he skips or guesses at. The student will often recognize the word once he has spelled it and noticed all of the letters.

### Neurological Impress Reading[16] to Increase Reading Accuracy and Attention to Meaning

Parents want to help their kids but often do not have the knowledge or patience to really teach their dyslexic learner. This simple, powerful technique is something that parents can easily do to make a real difference if done just ten minutes a day.

### *Neurological Impress Reading technique*

The instructor or parent sits next to or across from the student. The instructor points to each word with a finger above the word, and the student points below the word. Read *slowly* together using appropriate phrasing and intonation. It is okay if the student says the word after the instructor, but he must accurately say each word while pointing to it. Tap twice at each punctuation mark.

This technique improves orientation and synchrony between what the student is seeing and saying when reading. It takes the stress out of reading and keeps students from practicing reading words incorrectly. Neurological Impress Reading helps break the phonics-bound, sound-by-sound decoding that often keeps dyslexic students from reading fluently, and it allows students to focus on the meaning of each word and phrase, thus improving comprehension.

### *Independent Neurological Impress Reading with visualizing at punctuation*

The student points to each word and reads slowly using appropriate phrasing and intonation. If the student does not know a word, she should spell, then read the word. The instructor should supply the word if the student still does not know it after spelling it.

The student will tap twice at each punctuation mark. The instructor will question the student to see if she has created a mental image from the phrase or sentence just read. Do as much or as little questioning as needed to be sure that the student is imaging as she is reading. This will interrupt the flow of the reading at first, but gradually, the student will be able to mentally check her own images at each punctuation mark, without having to stop and discuss them.

This is a powerful technique to use individually with struggling readers, but it can also be used in groups to improve attention to words and meaning. Once students learn this technique, encourage them to use it on tests (reading silently to themselves), as it will improve their accuracy and comprehension when reading test questions and instructions.

### Integrate the Brain for Reading and Writing

Students with dyslexia and other learning challenges need help getting both sides of their brains and bodies working together. In fact, we all think and learn best when we have all of our resources working for us. These techniques can help students reset, re-energize, and get integrated for clearer thinking and learning.

# TAKE THE STONE OUT OF THE SHOE

### *Lazy 8s*

A Lazy 8 is a lying-down 8 like the infinity sign. Walking in a Lazy 8 pattern becomes a mental power walk that takes just a minute or two and has big benefits in calming frustration and anxiety and clearing and focusing the mind for learning.

### *Lazy 8s for writing*

The Lazy 8 for writing is a pencil and paper exercise geared toward improving writing skills. To do a Lazy 8, draw a sideways 8 on paper or a chalkboard with a flowing continuous movement. Start at the middle and draw counterclockwise first, up to the left and around; then clockwise, up and around to the right. This gets both hemispheres of the brain activated for thinking and writing.

Students who have trouble getting started on writing tasks can put a tiny Lazy 8 centered at the top of their paper and trace it several times to activate and integrate for writing.

## Classroom/Homework Spelling Tips and Accommodations for Supporting Dyslexic Students

### *How do you spell . . . ?*

Dyslexic students may become very dependent upon others for spelling, constantly asking their parent or teacher, "How do you spell . . . (fill in the blank)?"

### *Look up and spell it fast*

If your student asks you how to spell a sight word, particularly a non-phonetic word that you are pretty sure he knows, have him "look up and spell it fast." Looking up helps him access his visual memory, and spelling it fast helps him rely on what he already knows versus overthinking or sounding it out.

### *Say and write*

The student should say each sound *as* he writes it. This keeps him from guessing and being impulsive. It helps him think about all of the sounds in the word.

The vowel + *e* pattern is particularly tricky for many students, even if they can verbally explain the rule. Try having the student write the vowel + *e* as a single code as he says the sound, and then insert the consonant. This way he won't forget the silent *e,* and the pattern becomes more ingrained in his mind.

Example: For the word *make*, the student would say and write the following:

/m/ **m**

/ae/ m a **e**

/k/ ma**k**e

### *Proofreading for spelling*

Spelling requires both the ability to process the number, order, and identity of sounds in words, as well as the visual sequential memory capacity to retain what words look like. When checking their spelling, students should check to see if the word "sounds" right and looks right."

Checking spelling starting at the end of the sentence or paragraph and working forward takes the words out of context, making it easier to focus on each word.

# TAKE THE STONE OUT OF THE SHOE

### *Don't penalize for spelling*

Teachers: Don't penalize for spelling errors on content area assignments or tests. Students should always be expected to put forth their best effort on spelling and proofreading their work, but dyslexic students often know and understand so much more than their written work would indicate.

### *Spelling tests*

For severely dyslexic students, give them a greatly reduced list but require them to get as many letters as they can in the remaining words, at minimum, the first sound. This keeps them engaged for the whole spelling test and makes them less "different" while working on appropriate skills.

### *Visualize! Strategy for practicing spelling words*

To be a good speller, you must be able to think about the sounds in the word *and* have a mental picture of what the word looks like.

Here is a fun strategy for visualizing how words look.

1. Look at the word.

2. Look up and visualize the word on a large imaginary screen slightly above eye level. The letters should be large.

3. Point to each letter in the air and say the letter. Repeat three times to get a clear image of the word. (Draw the letters with two fingers if needed in order to get a good image.)

4. Now point to and say the letters in random order as fast as you can. (If the student can do this rapidly, he is getting a good image of the word.)

5. If there are tricky letters that the student tends to miss or make mistakes on, have him make those letters especially large, bright, or colorful in his image.

6. Spell the word forward and say the word.

Use this to practice difficult spelling words. Break the word into parts if needed and then put it back together and practice the whole word.

---

[14] Learning Ally efficacy studies are available at www.learningally.org.

[15] The Spell-Read strategy has been adapted from the Davis Reading Correction strategy detailed in *The Gift of Learning* (2003) by Ronald Davis.

[16] Neurological Impress Reading is a technique adapted by Dr. Joan Smith and included in EDU-Therapeutics training programs (edu-therapeutics.com).

Original research: Heckleman, R.G. "A Neurological Impress Method of Remedial Instruction," Academic Therapy, Volume: 4 issue: 4, pages 277-282, June 1969.

Chapter Fourteen
# DYSGRAPHIA AND WRITING

## Is Handwriting Important?

Is teaching handwriting a waste of time? One might think so in this digital age, but think again! Handwriting has a physiological and psychological link in the brain that impacts integration, attention, fluency, and learning. With a built-in capacity to regulate the emotional energy flow, the repetitive, multisensory stimulation of handwriting skills training impacts the emotional brain to reduce anxiety, increase motivation, and gain impulse control[17]

Handwriting is a complex perceptual motor skill.[18] It involves the following skills, any of which can cause graphomotor problems if not fully developed:

- **Visual-perceptual skills:** the ability to visually discriminate between written symbols such as letters and numbers and judge whether or not they are correct. These challenges are seen in reading and writing problems involving letter reversals and confusion with visually similar letters and words.
- **Orthographic coding:** the ability to hold a mental image of the printed word in memory; to store and retrieve letters, words, and word patterns. Students who have poor orthographic coding may forget how

to form letters in the middle of a writing task. They often trace over letters, have false starts as they write, and form letters in different ways.

- **Motor planning and execution:** the ability to plan, organize, and carry out movements in the right order. Students with dyspraxia, or poor motor planning and execution, have poor motor coordination and inefficient pencil grip. They may complain that their hand hurts when they write.

- **Kinesthetic feedback:** feedback from the body and movement that helps the student adjust and match their (mental) motor plan with the execution. Students with impaired kinesthetic feedback may grip the pencil too tightly or press too hard in order to get more kinesthetic input from their hand. They may prefer mechanical pencils and scratchy pens because they cause more friction on the paper and therefore more feedback. They may get their eyes very close to the page in order to guide their hand through visual versus kinesthetic feedback. This causes them to have to write much more slowly.

- **Visual-motor coordination:** eye-hand coordination, the ability to control hand movement guided by vision. Handwriting is fine-tuned by kinesthetic feedback, but visual feedback provides gross monitoring that helps students to be aware of margins, lines, and the edge of the paper when writing.

- **Graphomotor challenges**: Difficulty with handwriting is often overlooked as being a *real* problem and is poorly understood. Students with graphomotor problems are seen as lazy or unmotivated or oppositional because they resist doing work that requires writing. They are often accused of writing neatly when they "want to" because they may be able to do so if they write slowly enough. However, writing at a reasonable pace is not an option for them, causing homework to take hours and often making it impossible for them to keep up with the demands of the class.

### Alphabet 8s with Weights

This activity develops flow across the vertical midline, gets both hemispheres of the brain working together for writing, and improves stability and accuracy with letter formation.

Do Alphabets 8s[19] daily and watch graphomotor control and legibility improve!

### *Here's how to do it:*

On a board or large piece of paper, draw a large, very round Lazy 8 (lying on its side like the infinity sign). Draw a line up the midline of the 8.

Using the dominant hand, the student starts in the middle of the 8 and traces it going up and to the left first.

The student should put his non-dominant hand under the 8 at the midline and trace the 8 three times.

The student then writes each lowercase letter in printing, superimposed on the correct side of the 8. Each letter should be as large as the circles of the 8. Have the student say the letter name and the letter sound as he writes it.

Write each letter one time followed by tracing three full cycles of the 8 (starting in the middle and going up and to the left) before printing the next letter. Continue for the entire alphabet.

*Coaching:*

It may be helpful to have a written model of the alphabet for the student to check for letter formation. A chart with each letter printed on a Lazy 8 would also be helpful for some students.

Letters drawn on the left circle of the Lazy 8: *a, c, d, e, f, g, o, q, s, u, y.*

Letters starting on the midline and drawn on the right circle of the Lazy 8: *b, h, k, m, n, p, r, v, w, x, z.*

The letters *i, j, l,* and *t* are drawn on the midline.

Be sure the student is looking at his hand as he writes. He should follow the movement with his eyes, not his head.

Alphabet 8s are a Brain Gym activity. Charts are available through www.braingym.org.

### *Wrist weights*

To increase kinesthetic input and body awareness, have the student wear 1/4-pound wrist weights as they do Alphabet 8s.

### Handwriting Without Tears Paper Produces Improved Writing

Handwriting Without Tears [20] (HWT) is a multisensory program for teaching printing and handwriting. The lined paper used in this program has been valuable to our struggling writers, helping them more consistently and accurately size and space their letters.

The catch here is that the paper has to be used correctly, which takes coaching and monitoring for a while. Once the student becomes automatic with using the HWT paper and noticing and controlling the size and spacing of letters and words when writing, he can transition to using regular lined notebook paper

Here is an example of how HWT paper should be used. Notice that the body of lowercase letters fills the inside of the double line, with the *sticks* and *tails* above and below the lines, respectively.

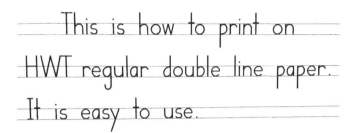

### 5-Minute Power Writing Strategy
*Principles:*
- It is easier to write from a question than a statement.
- The faster you write, the better you write.
- This gives you a way to break writing into small manageable chunks so it doesn't drag or feel overwhelming.

*Rules:*
- Start with three power words (nouns or verbs) about the topic.
- The first word in your first paragraph must be one of the three power words.
- The other two words must appear in the first paragraph.
- Write for five minutes without stopping. No editing erasing, or going back. No stopping to think.

*Steps:*
- Take your main idea sentence or topic and turn it into a question.
- Visualize the answer to the question.
- Write three power words (nouns or verbs) that will help answer the question.

- Write for five minutes following the rules.
- At the end of five minutes, edit, extend, and clarify the sentences.

Proofread with COPS.

## Proofreading Strategy–COPS

Here's a simple technique to help writers of any age become more willing and independent in proofreading their written work.

Have the student write COPS on a 3x5 card or at the top of her paper. Explain what each letter in the acronym stands for and walk through the process together with everything the student writes–even single sentences. Very quickly, most students will begin to apply COPS all on their own.

COPS stands for:

- **C**apitalization
- **O**verall appearance (spacing; clean, clear, well-formed letters; mistakes erased completely)
- **P**unctuation
- **S**pelling (Have the student check spelling by starting with the last word in the sentence or paragraph. This takes the words out of context. The student should check to see if the word sounds right and looks right).

Have students go through each sentence checking for capitalization. When done, they get to check off the C. Then check for overall appearance, checking it off when done. Go on to punctuation, followed by spelling.

[17] Further information about the connection between emotional regulation, attention, learning, and handwriting can be found in Training the Brain to Pay Attention the Write Way (1991) by Jeannette Farmer

[18] Dotterer, Cheri L. MS, OTR/L. Dysgraphia © 2018

[19] Alphabet 8s are a Brain Gym activity. Brain Gym is a comprehensive and effective series of activities that help integrate the brain for learning. Products and information available at www.braingym.org.

[20] Handwriting Without Tears programs and paper available through Learning Without Tears: www.lwt.com.

Chapter Fifteen
# COMPREHENSION AND MEMORY

## Comprehension and Memory Strategies

### *Visualize on the walls*

When teaching new information, discussing events in a story, or learning a sequence of steps or new vocabulary, guide students in developing mental images and locating them in order on various places on the walls. Then go back and drill or have them retell the information by looking at their images on the walls. Anchoring an image somewhere specific in space will make it easier to retrieve the information.

### *Associations*

Guide students in creating sequences of mental images to remember lists and facts (such as states and capitals, presidents, and steps in science or math formulas). Link each new image to the one before it.

Strong images are easier to remember. Students can make their images strong by adding color or movement, changing the size, making them silly or absurd, or making them illustrate a strong emotion.

Associations can be used to remember vocabulary or facts. Take, for example, this association for the term vagus nerve.

**Vagus nerve**: sometimes called the *vagabond nerve* because it connects so extensively in the body.

The student could visualize a vagabond walking along the "nerve highways" holding a stick on his shoulder with a knapsack on the end of it.

### *Rafter words*

Write difficult vocabulary or spelling words that students need to know in large, bold printed letters on cards and put them around your room up high on the wall. (Tip: Blue painter's tape will stick but not damage your walls). When students need to spell one of those words, have them look up and find it. Looking up and finding it in a specific location each time will help them imprint the word in their visual memory. This also works with other important information that needs to be memorized, such as the periodic table of elements.

### Concept Diagramming for Comprehension and Test Study

Most students have no idea how to study for a test. They often resort to reading the chapter over and over, hoping it will sink in; depending on parents to read the material and quiz them; or just hoping they somehow got the information through osmosis.

Some students work hard to memorize their study guides or practice questions word for word. They think they know the material, but when it appears on the test, stated in a different way, they don't recognize it as being what they studied and end up being disappointed in their grade.

## TAKE THE STONE OUT OF THE SHOE

Here is a strategy that takes a bit of time up front but helps students really understand the material and makes studying much more interesting. Test grades improve because students are really *thinking* about the information instead of just trying to ingest it by rote.

This strategy, called *concept diagramming*, is great for use with content areas such as history or science. It is a good tool to use when studying in groups or with a partner (or parent).

### Steps

The student should do the following:

1. Put important events, dates, vocabulary, and names on 3x5 cards.

2. Organize the cards in some way and orally explain why it makes sense to group the cards in that way.

3. Then mix the cards up and group them in another way, orally explaining the new connections.

4. After each test, save all of the cards, labeling them by chapter or section so they can be used again to study for unit tests and finals.

Be sure students organize the cards in at least two different ways and verbalize their thinking each time. This cements the concepts, relationships, and vocabulary. With this strategy, students are no longer memorizing by rote, but actively thinking about the information.

Chapter Sixteen
# DYSCALCULIA AND MATH

## Number Line

The number line is one of the most basic and valuable concepts for understanding how math works. People often think of a number line as simply a counting tool, but if your child or students do not understand math, this is the place to start.

The number line provides a visual springboard for learning about whole numbers, counting, addition (moving forward), subtraction (moving backward), greater than and less than, skip counting as an introduction to multiplication, division, fractions, decimals, and rational numbers. Most key math concepts can be explored on the number line.

As students work with the number line, they will develop number concepts and move away from strictly rote learning through experiencing and verbalizing. They should touch, use manipulatives, draw, and visualize the number line, talking through exactly what they are doing as they do it.

This kind of math dialoguing is a powerful tool to extend to all aspects of math. It helps students think through the sequence and logic of math computations. Have students prove, double-check, and give rationale for their answers, talking through each step.

## Math Dialoguing Technique

Math dialoguing is an excellent technique for teaching and reviewing computation processes. Students who learn to verbalize each step as they work will be more accurate and consistent in their math performance. They will be more likely to catch and correct their errors.

*Steps:*

1. The instructor does the computation problem, verbalizing and writing each step.

2. The instructor verbalizes as the student writes.

3. The student verbalizes as the instructor writes.

4. The student verbalizes and writes each step in the problem.

## Dealing with Those Dreaded Word Problems

Most parents I talk to dread word problems almost as much as their children do. Even if their child can do the rest of the math homework, the word problems often pose a problem. There are two main reasons for this:

1. The child has a reading problem and word problems require reading, or

2. The child (and parent) is trying to solve the problem by picking out the numbers or key words without really understanding what the problem is about.

Word problems are the application of math, the part that makes math something real and relevant. They used to be called *story* problems, and that's how we have to think of them—as a story. You don't just pick out the pieces you want from a story. If you do that, the story won't make sense. The best way to really understand a story is to visualize it, turning it into a movie in your head.

*Word problem strategy[21]*

1. Read and visualize the story. (Do one sentence at a time if necessary.)

2. Have your child talk about what he/she pictured. Who was in it? What were they doing? What were they trying to find out?

3. Use the chart below to think through the information. Have your child say what he's thinking as he goes. This helps him reason through the information and develop the language that he eventually will internalize and use on his own whenever doing word problems.

| QUESTION (What do I know)? | ? (What do I need to know)? | HOW (Solve the problem). |
|---|---|---|
| Here, write the relevant information in as few words as possible. | Write the question you have to solve for. | Do the math. Be sure to label the answer. |

Here is a simple problem as an example, but this strategy works with word problems of almost any level and helps students understand what they are doing:

**Problem:** Sara and Kaitlyn were on the same swim team. On Friday morning, Sara swam 19 laps and Kaitlyn swam 23 laps. How many more laps did Kaitlin swim than Sara?

Visualize and verbalize (make a mental movie) of the story:

"I picture two girls in a swimming pool swimming laps. They both swam a lot of laps, but Sara got out after 19 laps, and Kaitlin kept going until she completed 23 laps. I have to figure out how many laps Kaitlin did after Sara got out of the pool."

To solve this, you might have to guide your child in recognizing that until Sara got out of the pool, the two girls swam the same number of laps. The *difference* is the number of laps Kaitlin swam once Sara got out. Whenever you are finding the difference, you will subtract the smaller number from the larger number.

| WHAT | ? | HOW |
|---|---|---|
| S: 19 laps<br>K: 23 laps | How many more laps did Kaitlin swim than Sara? | 23<br>-19<br>4 laps |

Have your child verbalize or write the full answer to the problem:

Kaitlin swam four more laps than Sara.

This takes some time at first, but the more you do it, the more independent and confident your child will get with word problems.

# TAKE THE STONE OUT OF THE SHOE

## Math Triangles (+ − x ÷ Facts)

Purpose:

- Help students associate addition and subtraction as opposite operations
- Help students associate multiplication and division as opposite operations
- Learn math facts

Procedure:

- Make flashcards of challenging math facts (those that the student doesn't know and needs to practice). Draw a triangle on the card.

- For addition and subtraction (+/-) put the answer to the addition problem (sum) at the top of the triangle. On the bottom two corners, put the addends (two numbers that are added together to make the sum).

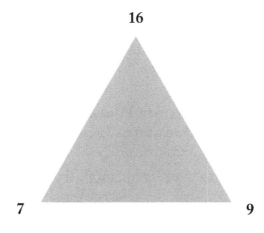

- Have the student practice reading all possible problems as the instructor points to the numbers:

  7 + 9 = 16

  9 + 7 = 16

  16 − 7 = 9

  16 − 9 = 7

- Guide the student in noting:
  - Whichever order he adds the numbers at the bottom of the triangle, the answer is always the same.
  - The answer (sum) of an addition problem is always a bigger number than either of the two numbers he is adding.
  - When subtracting, he always starts with the biggest number (16 in the problem above).
  - The relationship between the addition and subtraction facts: that the addition and subtraction facts use the same numbers.
- Drill while looking at the numbers: The instructor points to the number. The student says the numbers and supplies the operation based on where the instructor started.
- Drill the various facts: Instructor covers one corner of the triangle and says the corresponding problem. The student says the answer.
- Drill with a visualized triangle: The instructor points to the spot where the numbers would be as the student says the numbers and supplies the operation based on where the instructor started.

## For multiplication and division (x ÷)

- The procedure and practice work the same for multiplication and division as for addition and subtraction. At the top of the triangle, put the answer to the multiplication problem (product). On the bottom two corners, put the *factors* (two numbers that are multiplied together to make the product).

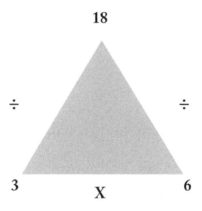

Signs can be added to the triangle as needed to help the student understand and remember.

## Memory Grid for Tough Multiplication Facts[22]

Purpose:
- To remember numeric combinations

- To use visualization and visual memory to recall information

Activity:

- Create a 3 x 3 grid on a paper.
- Fill in the numbers 1 through 9 on the grid.
- Have students memorize the numbers on the grid.
- Play tic-tac-toe with the grid from memory.
- Use the grid to place the times table combinations (1 x 3, 2 x 3, 3 x 3, etc.).
- Imagine the grid with the combinations.
- Drill/play tic-tac-toe to reinforce the grid.
- Imagine and drill with answers only, then with a blank grid.
- Use the grid concept for one or two of the most difficult sets of multiplication tables. (Often the 8s are very difficult for students to recall).

| 1 | 2 | 3 |
|---|---|---|
| 4 | 5 | 6 |
| 7 | 8 | 9 |

# TAKE THE STONE OUT OF THE SHOE

| 1 x 3 = 3 | 2 x 3 = 6 | 3 x 3 = 9 |
|---|---|---|
| 4 x 3 = 12 | 5 x 3 = 15 | 6 x 3 = 18 |
| 7 x 3 = 21 | 8 x 3 = 24 | 9 x 3 = 27 |

| 3 | 6 | 9 |
|---|---|---|
| 12 | 15 | 18 |
| 21 | 24 | 27 |

[21] Word problem strategy adapted from the Discover Math program by Dr. Steven Truch, Founding Director of the Reading Foundation. www.readingfoundation.com

[22] The Memory Grid was one of numerous practical hands-on strategies included in EDU-Therapeutics training programs (edu-therapeutics.com) developed by Dr. Joan Smith.

# Part 3: Real Solutions and the Science Behind Them

## *Introduction*

As a young special education teacher working with students with learning disabilities, I knew there had to be more that could be done for my students than simply holding their head above water in their school subjects and giving them accommodations that got them through but made them feel different and less capable.

By definition, a student with a diagnosed learning disability has at least average to above-average intelligence, so why were we giving these smart, creative students workarounds and tools for living with their learning challenges instead of finding ways to actually remove the roadblocks so they would be free to enjoy learning and reach their potential?

I left the public schools to find an answer to this question, and what an incredible journey it has been! I have had the opportunity to study with experts all over the world in the fields of neuroscience, attention, and learning–those innovative clinicians and researchers who push the edges of their field and the comfort zone of traditional education in order to understand how the brain learns and what is needed to optimize potential.

This section will give you hope based in truth–the science and clinical evidence.

We will look at some of the key programs that we use at Stowell Learning Centers to make the real and lasting changes we are looking for in our students. While double-blind research studies would be fantastic to have (and I certainly want the medical community to continue their practice of relying on this kind of research), the cost and time are prohibitive for the education field. However, following the guidelines of neuroscience, psychology, biology, science-driven research, and evidence-based clinical practices along with our own thirty-six years of targeted clinical experience, I can confidently assure you that the programs and strategies presented in this section work to permanently change or eliminate difficulties associated with dyslexia, learning, or attention challenges.

Chapter Seventeen
# WHAT DOES IT TAKE TO PERMANENTLY CORRECT A LEARNING CHALLENGE?

In her adult life, Jessica became a doctorate-level reading professor at a prestigious university. As a nine-year-old, she was a nonreader. The root of the problem was weak auditory processing that kept her brain from discriminating the differences in sounds and learning and using phonics for reading and spelling.

The traditional approach at school and in tutoring provided Jessica with phonics instruction and lots of reading practice. But it didn't work–not because of poor teaching, but because her brain couldn't access the information it needed to benefit from the instruction.

If we want to permanently change or correct a learning challenge, we must identify and develop the underlying foundational learning or processing skills that are the real reason the student is struggling. The brain is a learning machine, so once the pathways are open and the brain is getting the information it needs, it will learn.

## Identifying the Lagging Underlying Skills

Each student comes to our learning centers with their own unique set of strengths and challenges. In order to create the most targeted and effective plan for correcting their challenges, we do what we call a Functional Academic and Learning Skills Assessment. This is different than a psycho-educational assessment that may be done at school in order to qualify a student for special services.

Our goal is not to qualify or specifically provide a diagnosis for a student, but to get a clear functional view of what the challenges look like: Which of the underlying skill areas are weak? How does that specifically impact the student's academic functioning, social skills, behavior, attention, and self-management?

The Functional Academic and Learning Skills Assessment includes both formal standardized tests as well as informal functional tests and observations. Testing may evaluate both basic academic skills and underlying neurodevelopmental, processing, and executive function skills. Parent and student input provide very important information in understanding and programming for the student.

### Targeted Plan and Training

Taking into account the goals of the parent and student, a targeted plan is created for the student to develop the underlying neurodevelopmental, processing, and executive function skills along with remediation of the affected basic academic skills (reading, writing, comprehension, spelling, and math).

The plan may include more than one step, as the development of underlying skills is often sequential and, in most cases, involves a number of different skills.

Recommended programs and strategies are what are called *neuroplastic interventions*.[23] Brain research in the last forty years has proven that the brain has *neuroplasticity*, or the ability to develop new neural connections and pathways as the result of intensive and targeted training. Neuroplastic interventions along with sound teaching techniques pave the way for permanent changes for struggling learners.

## The Importance of Frequency and Intensity

There are many ways to implement student programs, and we never want parents to feel that because of financial or time constraints, it is impossible for them to get their child the help they need. In most cases, when it comes to using neuroplastic interventions to address a learning challenge, some is better than none.

All of that being said, frequency and intensity of instruction are powerful pieces of correcting learning challenges or learning anything well.

Researcher and program developer Patricia Lindamood described the need for frequency to me in this way: Imagine playing baseball on a field of grass where no one has ever played before. You lay your bases down and run around them once or twice. Does a pathway suddenly appear? No, of course not. It takes frequently and consistently running between bases over and over to establish a solid pathway. Unless the new learning or experience is imprinted permanently on the brain by some tumultuous event or emotion, frequency is a key in establishing a new learning, habit, or function.

Intensity is an important piece of cognitive training of underlying learning skills. Not only do you need to be working on the right skills, but also you have to push the learner to the edge of their comfort zone. The things that stretch us the most will make the greatest change in the brain.

## Time

Correcting learning challenges, including dyslexia, takes time. It is a process. It is not a magic pill, but thankfully, it is not a forever process either. When students start our cognitive learning therapy, I know that there will be a period of time where they are still struggling in school and taking hours to do their homework while they are starting to correct the problem. I also know they just need to hang in there. With consistency, things will change. The gap will begin to close. Making these kinds of permanent changes in learning just takes time.

Most of our students spend nine to twenty-four months with us, but depending upon the number and severity of challenges and the number of hours per week that a student can attend, it may be more. What we're after is life changing!

Recently, a parent asked a very relevant question: "If this is working, why is my child still failing in school? Can't you just work on his schoolwork?"

The student in question is twelve years old and has very weak auditory and visual processing, reading, writing, and spelling skills. He has good comprehension and memory, which he relied on in the primary grades, but the demands of sixth grade are just too great. His weak skills make it impossible for him to do the following:

- Get all of the information taught in class
- Take good notes
- Get his assignments written accurately in his planner
- Read assignments well enough to really understand them
- Express himself on paper

- Read test questions correctly
- Complete tests in the time allotted

Helping this student with schoolwork may allow him to pass his classes by the skin of his teeth, but at the end of the school year, nothing will have changed. The same learning challenges will exist. If we want to make a real impact on this boy's chances as a student, we have to go after the underlying skills that are causing him to struggle in the first place.

## Programming

The brain has always been a fascinating subject, and clinical researchers worldwide have been studying the brain and learning for decades. The programming we use to help children and adults resolve their learning and attention challenges and truly reach their potential has been learned and compiled from the work of these incredible people.

The plan for each individual student is most often a combination of programs and strategies sequenced to develop the neurodevelopmental (Core Learning Skills), processing, executive function, and basic academic skills needed to bring that student to the point of being the most comfortable and independent learner he or she has the potential to be. After thirty-six years and having worked with thousands of students both onsite and remotely, we know that it is absolutely possible to make these changes and it never gets old!

The remainder of this section will be devoted to sharing some of the key programs that we use at Stowell Learning Centers. The majority of these programs, both those created at Stowell Learning Centers and those developed by others, are implemented on a one-to-one basis and require training and certification in order to provide them. As you search for help for your child, look for therapists/providers who offer these programs or programming that addresses the underlying skills at the root of the challenges as well as sound basic academic remediation.

23 Doidge, Norman. *The Brain's Way of Healing: Remarkable Dscoveries and Recoveries from the Frontiers of Neuroplasticity.* USA: Penguin Books, 2016.

Chapter Eighteen
# MUSIC-BASED AUDITORY TRAINING

Imagine watching your favorite movie without the music. It just wouldn't be the same. Music has been scientifically proven to have a powerful impact on the brain and emotions. At Stowell Learning Centers, we use music-based auditory training, or sound therapy, to develop not only auditory processing but also to support all aspects of learning.

The brain is wired for sound. Music can literally change neurochemistry, boost mood and immune function, and reduce stress without the side effects of drugs. Music and sound have a powerful impact on learning, communication, behavior, relationships, sleep, and sense of well-being. Auditory training, or sound therapy, is a powerful tool that facilitates the development of auditory processing and supports virtually every other type of training we do with our students. The music opens up doors in the brain that we simply cannot get to otherwise.

## Sound Frequencies

The human brain can process a wide spectrum of sound frequencies ranging from 20 to 20,000 hertz. Different sound frequencies affect our function and behavior in different ways. Both music tempo (beats per minute) and sound frequencies entrain with the brain, making it possible to use sound and music as a therapeutic tool.

**Lower frequencies** can be thought of as the "body sounds." Low-frequency sounds and slower tempos stimulate lower brain functions, supporting calming, grounding, and regulation.

Aiden was a difficult child. When I first met him, he was five, extremely bright, and precocious. He was fun and impressive for the first few minutes. Then, when his mom and dad talked to me a moment too long, Aiden got very agitated and started pulling relentlessly on his parents, who, of course, were mortified. Every effort they made to calm him drove up his and their anxiety level and fight-or-flight responses.

The following Monday, Aiden started a home listening program targeting low frequencies. He listened fifteen minutes twice a day. On Friday that week, his mom called to ask if Aiden could continue listening over the weekend instead of taking the recommended two days off because it was making such a difference for him and the family. In his first week of listening, Aiden was decidedly calmer and more agreeable. That Sunday, he attended Sunday school for the first time in months without the typical mishaps and meltdowns that had caused him to have to be removed from the class.

Aiden worked with us at the learning center for a little over a year. His sensory processing issues were not going to be corrected in a week, but starting his program with the organizing, grounding influence of low-frequency auditory training opened the door for change.

**Mid-range frequencies** are the "learning sounds." Most speech sounds fall in this frequency range. Challenges processing mid-range frequencies can impact learning, communication, comprehension, reading, emotional regulation, and social skills.

Ellie was six when her teacher referred her to the learning center. Ellie was a coordinated, friendly little girl who was very difficult to understand because of her limited language and poor articulation. She seemed completely lost in class and was struggling to learn to read. Trying to get her to do homework was a daily trauma.

We can only reproduce the sounds that the brain can "hear" or process. If we have disordered auditory processing, the brain will not get a clear message. If we don't understand the messages coming in, it's hard to express an accurate response to those messages. Ellie had disordered auditory processing.

Language and music are made up of sound frequencies, so music gives us a way to train the brain to process language sounds. The mid-range frequencies touch Wernicke's and Broca's areas in the brain, which are associated with expressive language and speech, respectively.

Ellie's listening program was focused on stimulating the mid-range frequencies. Her dad reported, "Within a month, two months, she was making the kind of progress we didn't expect she could make for years." Two years later, Ellie was reading at grade level, doing schoolwork and homework independently, and "interacting with all of her peers" in her general education class. Her dad said the only thing standing in the way of Ellie doing her homework then was that she had become an avid reader and didn't want to put down her book!

**High frequencies** are energizing to the cortex of the brain, stimulating alertness, focus, and motivation. These are the frequencies that add detail and definition to sound, making it easier to discriminate sounds in words and intonation in the voice. Low energy; brain fog or slow thinking; feeling down, depressed, or unmotivated; not picking up subtle cues in intonation; and unclear or monotone speech can be related to poor processing of high-frequency sounds.

I remember teaching an auditory training seminar, and a therapist who was attending said, "Wow! I think my son needs this!" Alan was in his first year of college. His mom said that he was smart and very talented in music and sports, but all through high school, he had been moody and unmotivated. He never reached his potential or developed his talents. He didn't have friends, and he quit everything. In fact, while his mom was at the seminar, he dropped out of college.

We got him started on a listening program with an emphasis on higher frequencies. Three weeks in, he shared with me that he had always been up and down mood-wise, but mostly down, and he said, "But now, I'm mostly up!"

He was really excited because someone he had met at college called and asked if he wanted to get together with some other friends. As though he couldn't quite believe it, he said, "And I went! They acted like they liked me–like I was a leader!"

I ran into Alan's mom a couple of years later at another seminar, and she said that listening had had such a profound impact on Alan that he said, "I'm a listener for life!"

### Auditory Zoom

Dr. Alfred Tomatis, French physician and pioneer in the field of auditory processing and sound therapy, discovered that the ear is not a passive organ. The ear has the ability to tune in or tune out noises, almost like a zoom lens on a camera. In fact, Tomatis called this function *auditory zoom*.[24] This is a critical factor for attention and listening, as it allows us to focus on particular sounds, such as a teacher's voice, and filter out others, such as classroom noise.

Auditory zoom is accomplished through the workings of the two tiniest muscles in the body—the *stapedius* and *tensor tympani* muscles in the middle ear. These are regulated by the brain and work automatically and unconsciously most of the time, but when we intentionally listen to a particular conversation, we are actively influencing the workings of these muscles.

The job of the stapedius muscle is to increase the perception and discrimination of the mid to high frequencies in language while dampening the lower frequencies in background noise that would mask or overwhelm the higher-frequency sounds. This allows us to tune in to language in the environment. The tensor tympani, which adjusts the tension in the eardrum, works alongside the stapedius to reduce the perception of low-frequency sounds in background noise. The middle ear muscles also provide a protective function, contracting when we speak and in the presence of loud noises to prevent injury to the ears.

Dr. Tomatis found that when the middle ear muscles don't work well because they are weak, as is the case for many children with autism, learning disabilities, and speech and language delays, the person cannot tune in to the frequencies of speech because their middle ears muscles are not working properly to dampen the low frequencies from the background environment. This makes it difficult to get a clear, complete, accurate message when listening because instead of discriminating specific frequencies, the perceived sound is muffled or a mash of undifferentiated sound.

Weakness in the stapedius and tensor tympani is often seen in children who have had chronic ear infections and those who experience hypotonia (generalized low muscle tone), which is common in children with developmental delays.

Studies by Jonathan Fritz[25] and his colleagues at the University of Maryland show that neuroplasticity applies to auditory zoom. The function and regulation of the middle ear muscles, desire to listen, and processing of sound frequencies can successfully be trained through sound therapy.

## Neurological Connections and Sound Therapy/Auditory Training

Cranial nerve 10 (CN X), the vagus nerve, has connections to the external ear as well as to nearly every organ and function in the body. The central auditory nervous system (CANS) transmits sound signals from the ear through the brain stem, midbrain, and cortex, impacting auditory attention, discrimination, pattern recognition, emotion, and language. The vestibulocochlear nerve (CN IIX) transmits information about hearing and balance to the brain.

Because of the vast neurological connections between the ear and other functions in the body and brain, sound has an impact not only on language and learning but also on attention, emotional regulation, speech, energy, mood, balance, movement, and overall sense of safety and well-being. This makes sound therapy an extraordinary tool for improving numerous aspects of learning and functioning.

In the 1950s, Tomatis explored how to use music and sound to train the auditory system. At first, he worked with opera singers, but then he began to apply his findings to other issues, including dyslexia. Since that time, a number of therapeutic listening programs have been developed to train auditory processing. Currently in our centers, we use listening programs developed by Advanced Brain Technologies (ABT) and Integrated Listening Systems (iLs).

This kind of music-based auditory training is one of the single most powerful tools we use. The science of sound and the neurology of the auditory system, all those connections between the body, the brain, and the ear, make it possible to use specially recorded, acoustically modified music to improve auditory processing as well as sensory processing, executive function, organization, short-term memory, learning skills, focus, mood, and sleep.

Training the auditory system allows it to process information that it wasn't tuning in to before. I remember a very quiet, socially and academically delayed sixteen-year-old who came to us for a summer intensive program. She started her sound therapy program, and at the end of her first week, her mom was noticing that she was more aware of conversations in the home and was interested and engaging in a way that she had not done before. It was as though she suddenly woke up. This was the beginning of a journey that, along with her cognitive learning therapy, unlocked her potential and saw her move out of a special education classroom into the mainstream, make friends, and go on to college after graduation

### The Listening Program (TLP) and inTime

TLP and inTime are auditory training programs (sound therapy) developed by Advanced Brain Technologies (ABT). Advanced Brain Technologies[26] and its founder Alex Doman are dedicated to improving brain performance and learning through the application of neurotechnology.

TLP encompasses several programs of music and sound stimulation that focus on re-educating the ear and auditory pathways for increased learning, attention, communication, listening, sensory integration, and physical coordination. This is accomplished through the use of specially recorded and engineered classical music and nature sounds that stimulate the auditory system to tune in to auditory input and take in a full spectrum of sound frequencies.

inTime adds the components of percussion and rhythm to the frequency-based auditory training.

Students do their listening program with high-quality over-the-ear headphones or with WAVES, a multi-sensory audio headphone system with bone conduction technology combined with air conduction, which was created by Advanced Brain Technologies.

We have two natural modes of hearing–through our ears (air conduction) and through our bones (bone conduction). Studies and our experience have shown that adding bone conduction to a listening program is particularly helpful for students who need stronger input or have significant challenges with physical or emotional regulation or confidence.

Different sound frequencies relate to different regions in the brain and their associated functions. Music provides us a tool for training the different brain regions. Color-coded frequency zones are used in the ABT listening programs to improve awareness and attention to different sound frequency ranges and to stimulate various brain regions and functions.

The Green Zone uses music with a slower tempo (fewer beats per minute) and lower frequencies (20–1,500 HZ) that are grounding and calming to the nervous system and integrate the lower brain areas.

The Orange Zone focuses on mid-range frequencies (1,500–5,000 HZ) and moderate tempos. The Orange Zone relates to attention, focus, communication, and learning,

The higher frequencies (5,000–20,000 HZ) and faster tempos of the Red Zone relate to frontal lobe executive functions, spatial orientation, planning, creativity, and working memory skills.

Students can also benefit from training the entire brain. TLP protocols begin with the Blue Zone, which is full-spectrum music that gently trains across all of the sound frequencies. This eases the learner into the auditory training and provides a base to build upon. The Green Zone is trained next in order to strengthen the sensorimotor foundation and stress resilience. Then, communication skills are built with the Orange Zone, followed by the Red Zone for higher-order thinking.

The sound frequency progression in TLP follows the model of human child development. The young child first becomes physically efficient. Once we have that physical efficiency, we begin to develop receptive and expressive language and communication skills. With the basics of communication coming in, we begin to develop higher-order thinking with increasing complexity. TLP training progresses from the brain stem to the midbrain to the cortex and then trains back down, to achieve whole-brain training over time.

### Integrated Listening Systems (iLs)

iLs sound therapy programs were developed by Ron Minson, MD, and Integrated Listening Systems.[27] iLs is a home- or clinic-based listening program that is grounded in Tomatis' research and systems. It combines frequency-based training provided through air and bone conduction with physical activity.

Students listen forty to eighty minutes per day three or more days a week to a prescribed iLs protocol that gently and specifically activates the neural pathways for sensory processing.

iLs has both predetermined programs and the option for the provider to tailor the program more specifically to the individual listener. All programs are created around four phases of listening:

1. Organization

2. Transition

3. Activation

4. Integration

The Organization Phase uses full-spectrum music to ease the student into sound therapy and support grounding, regulation, and physical and mental organization. Based on the polyvagal theory,[28] or the science of feeling safe, the Organization Phase helps the student to feel safe and secure in order to be ready and open for more intense training.

During the Transition Phase, there is a gradual increase in filtered music and higher frequencies. Filtered music allows certain frequencies to be filtered out in order to increase or decrease the intensity and attention on the target frequency ranges in the music. iLs transitions the listener gradually from the lower grounding, organizing frequencies to the more intense and detailed mid-and high-range frequencies.

In the Activation Phase, the student listens to music that has been filtered to increase the brain's awareness of increasingly higher frequencies in order to stimulate communication, focus, thinking, and learning.

The Integration Phase helps the listener bring their awareness and processing of the higher frequencies that were isolated in the Activation Phase into full-spectrum music.

Students do their iLs listening with special over-the-ear headphones that provide the sound through both air and bone conduction. Bone conduction[29] massively engages the vestibular nuclei in the brain so that all parts of the body are stimulated. Because bone conduction influences the vestibular system, it helps improve spatial awareness, body organization, balance, and coordination.

Bone conduction is calming and grounding, balancing the energizing effects of high frequencies, which is particularly important for some of our more sensitive students.

iLs uses a variety of music types: orchestra, waltz, cello, and male and female chant. Choosing the music type allows us to tailor the protocol to the student's individual needs at that moment. A cello is a large instrument firmly planted on the ground that produces low tones. The cello can help a student with scattered thoughts or a constantly moving body begin to settle, center, and focus.

A student who tends to be very rigid may benefit from the ease and flow of the waltz.

Chant is a good choice for helping students feel secure and engaged. Chant is rhythmic and steady and uses human voice, all of which can be calming to the nervous system.

### Combining Listening and Movement

We often have students do movement activities, either their Core Learning Skills training or the iLs Playbook, while doing their sound therapy. Our eyes, ears, and vestibular system (balance and spatial orientation) must work closely together for optimal functioning to occur. These systems are vital to our ability to pay attention, coordinate movement, process information, and learn. These systems support each other, and training them together is effective in enhancing sensory integration.

### Safe and Sound Protocol (SSP)

SSP (core program) is a five-to ten-day listening intervention based on the polyvagal theory and developed by Dr. Stephen Porges and iLs. It is designed to reduce stress and auditory sensitivity while enhancing social engagement and resilience. We have found this protocol to be extremely effective in reducing the reactivity of students with highly volatile behavior, as well as reducing anxiety and bringing about a greater sense of ease, control, and confidence in children and adults who, for whatever reason, are operating in a high-alert state or with a high degree of anxiety.

The student listens to popular vocal music with comfortable rhythmic and intonation patterns that has been filtered to train the middle ear muscles to focus in on the frequency range of human speech. Once human speech is properly perceived, the portal to social engagement has been opened. The listener is better able to interpret meaning and intent in conversation.

[24] In his book, *The Brain's Way of Healing: Remarkable Discoveries and Recoveries from the Frontiers of Neuroplasticity*, Norman Doidge MD discusses auditory zoom and other aspects and discoveries of Tomatis' work with auditory processing and sound therapy in Chapter 8.

[25] Jonathan B. Fritz, Pingbo Yin, and Shihab A. Shamma. "Rapid Spectrotemporal Plasticity in Primary Auditory Cortex During Behavior," Journal of Neuroscience, March 2014.

[26] Information about Advanced Brain Technologies' (ABT) professional training, programs, and research can be found at www.advancedbrain.com.

[27] Information about Integrated Listening Systems' (iLs) professional training, programs, and research can be found at www.integratedlistening.com.

[28] The polyvagal theory proposed and researched by Dr. Stephen Porges looks at how the nervous system and body respond to a sense of safety or threat and how that impacts our behavior. The vagus nerve allows the brain to monitor what is happening in the body and determine how we react.

[29] Bone conduction information was learned through multiple trainings and talks given by Ron Minson, MD

JILL STOWELL

Chapter Nineteen
# AUDITORY STIMULATION AND TRAINING (AST)

When bright children and adults struggle with speaking, reading, comprehension, or spelling, it is almost always the result of weak underlying auditory, visual, and/or language processing skills that are not supporting the learner well enough. This means that in order to permanently correct these challenges, those critical supporting skills must be developed. More practice with academic skills is simply not enough.

Auditory Stimulation and Training is scientifically-based auditory training programming that uses a combination of sound therapy and specific evidence-based reading, language, or comprehension lessons to improve underlying skills critical to listening and reading success. Auditory processing skills are improved through sound therapy and audio-vocal training lessons that help the learner get clearer and more accurate information when listening. This impacts speech clarity, intonation, comprehension, verbal expression, and attention.

Lessons are structured to stimulate and improve visualization of information that is read or heard; working memory; grammar and word usage; phonological awareness, decoding, and spelling skills; reading accuracy, fluency, and comprehension; and reasoning skills for test taking and analyzing questions.

There are four unique and comprehensive Auditory Stimulation and Training (AST) Programs developed by Jill Stowell, founder of Stowell Learning Centers:

- AST-Reading and Spelling
- AST-Comprehension
- AST-Comprehension and Study Skills
- AST-Language

Each program has a strong auditory training base and addresses critical processing/learning skills in combination with targeted training in listening, speaking, reading, comprehension, and/or spelling.

The AST programs stimulate:
- Auditory awareness and processing of a full range of sound frequencies
- Auditory attention to higher frequencies in sound
- The voice to become an ongoing stimulus for the auditory system (auditory feedback loop)
- Improved self-monitoring of voice and content
- Right ear/left brain dominance for language and reading

### Passive Auditory Training

Sound therapy increases the brain's ability to pay attention to a wide range of frequencies in sound. The lower frequencies in sound are especially important for coordination, movement, rhythm, and organization. Mid-range frequencies are especially important for hearing and reproducing speech sounds. High-frequency sounds are energizing to the brain and are critical for attention, thinking, and learning. The high frequencies in sound also carry the detailed information that makes it possible to discriminate between similar speech sounds and words, tone of voice, and different instruments and voices.

The filtered music in sound therapy programs highlights or brings attention to sound frequencies that the listener was previously unable to discriminate. With the increased awareness, the brain and middle ear muscles begin to work harder to tune in to the higher frequencies in sound, particularly the language frequencies.

### Auditory Feedback Loop

In his research, Dr. Tomatis found that the voice cannot reproduce what the brain cannot hear. People who frequently mispronounce words, have low energy, get confused or misunderstand when listening, have difficulty sounding out words, or speak with poor inflection or a monotone voice typically have poor listening skills.

Once the brain is processing a greater range of frequencies in sound, the listener will have better energy and better input with which to think and learn. Audio-vocal training is used to help the student's voice acquire the wide range of frequencies that his brain is learning to hear or pay attention to.

When the voice is richer and contains a wider range of frequencies, it becomes the ongoing stimulus for the auditory system. This is called the *auditory feedback loop*.[30] This has many positive outcomes:

- Speaking now provides energy to the brain for thinking.
- The person is more interesting to listen to.

- Social and communication skills improve.
- The ability to hear one's voice more accurately allows the person to monitor her speaking, reading, and spelling accuracy.
- Singing improves.
- The person is better able to monitor his content and tone when he speaks.

### Feeding the Right Ear–Left Brain

Tomatis found that people tend to speak primarily out of one side of their mouth.[31] Those with good listening skills nearly always speak out of the right side of their mouth, constantly feeding the right ear the sounds of their speech. Since each brain hemisphere receives most of its sound input from the ear on the opposite side of the body, sound from the right ear goes to the left hemisphere for processing.

In most people, whether right or left-handed, the key elements of language are processed in the left hemisphere of the brain. Neurologically, there is a quicker, more direct connection between the right ear and the left hemisphere than from the left ear, making the right ear more efficient as the dominant ear for language.

When a person speaks out of the left side of their mouth, the sound of their voice is being directed to the left ear and a slower, more circuitous route to the left hemisphere. This can cause a delay in processing speech in real time and contribute to language, comprehension, speech, and reading delays. Speaking on the left side of the mouth and listening with the left ear can lead to disorganization in the brain that contributes to dyslexia and other learning and attention challenges.

# TAKE THE STONE OUT OF THE SHOE

## Reading on the Wrong Side of the Brain

In most people, the right hemisphere of the brain carries out little to no linguistic processing. Sometimes referred to as the *gestalt brain*, it tries to make sense of the whole as opposed to the individual parts. It helps us perceive whole visual forms, such as faces and shapes. Music, prosody, and non-linguistic sounds, such as slamming doors, car horns, and the wind in the trees, are processed and interpreted in the right hemisphere.

The right brain processes great amounts of information simultaneously and almost instantaneously. You look out the window and get a big-picture view of what's in that space and everything that is happening there all at once, as opposed to left-brain processing, which is generally sequential, one piece after another, like the sounds in language.

Research on dyslexia indicates that many dyslexic individuals engage the right side of the brain when reading.[32] This creates disorganization and confusion, as the right brain simply cannot process language in the way that the left hemisphere does. This causes them to make errors such as the following:

- Saying a word with a similar meaning when reading, such as *physician* for *doctor* or *house* for *home*. The right brain sees the word *home* as a shape related to a concept instead of a grouping of letters and sounds that say "home."

- Omitting periods and other punctuation marks as though they don't exist. These small pieces of language are not recognized by the right side of the brain as being important. In fact, they can be very disorienting to the dyslexic learner. An adult student once shared that punctuation marks were like gnats flying around the page. They were annoying and

bothersome to look at, and he had no idea why they were there.
- Adding, omitting, or changing word endings and small common words such as *the*, *of*, and *if* as they cannot conceptualize or imagine what they are.[33]
- Confusing visually similar words such as *quietly* and *quality* because the right brain sees a whole picture of a word as opposed to a sequence of letters and sounds.
- Having alarming short-term verbal memory deficits.
- Spelling bizarrely.
- Reading accurately but slowly and laboriously.

**Audio-Vocal Training**

Audio-vocal training is provided through directed, one-to-one instruction. The instructor's voice may be amplified with a microphone feeding into the student's headphones to give the student stronger input. The high frequencies are amplified slightly, and the low frequencies are slightly dampened in order to enhance the higher frequencies in the voice.

The student's voice is also amplified either with a microphone set up like the instructor's or with Forbrain Auditory Feedback Headphones. Forbrain enhances specific frequencies in speech and uses bone conduction to transmit the student's voice.

A third option for amplifying the student's voice, and one that we often use as a supplement to the student's program, is the "hand mic." This is free and effective! The student makes a fist with her right hand and holds it about an inch away from her mouth, turning her hand very slightly to the right. When she speaks, the sound will be amplified to her right ear. Lower frequencies will be dampened by the hand, enhancing the high frequencies going to the right ear.

Enhanced lateralization, a technique explored and developed by Dorothy van den Honert,[34] may be added to auditory training to increase right ear dominance for language and stimulate left hemisphere processing of language and reading. In this technique, the student receives verbal input through the right ear, and music in the left ear. The music, in a sense, "distracts" or occupies the right brain's attention while the language is processed by the left hemisphere.

Enhanced lateralization has been a highly successful technique with our students with dyslexia and expressive language delays.

**Auditory Stimulation and Training–Reading and Spelling (AST-R/S)**

AST-Reading and Spelling has sixty directed audio-vocal training lessons that specifically address the auditory skills needed for good listening and processing of auditory information. Critical underlying skills for reading and spelling are embedded into the lessons. Lessons take approximately fifty to sixty minutes and are designed to be provided by an instructor working one-to-one with the student three times per week.

*Processing skills developed:*

- Auditory processing skills, including auditory decoding, auditory memory, phonological awareness, and sound discrimination
- Visual processing skills, including visual attention, visual discrimination, visual memory, and visualization
- Phonological awareness skills, including segmenting, blending, and manipulating sounds and syllables in words

- Auditory-visual synchrony

*Language skills developed:*
- Articulation and pronunciation/verbal clarity
- Word usage: pronouns, prepositions, articles, verb tense, contractions, plurals, possessives
- Vocabulary
- Comprehension
- Intonation
- Fluency
- Discrimination of auditorily similar words
- Flexibility with word order and sentence structure
- Punctuation

*Reading skills developed:*
- Phonological awareness
- Consonant and vowel sounds and spelling patterns
- Phonetic decoding (simple, complex, and multisyllable)
- Visual decoding (quickly noticing and decoding logical visual letter groupings in words)
- Common and irregular word endings
- Phrasing
- Fluency
- Self-monitoring of intonation, fluency, and attention to meaning
- Comprehension

*Spelling and writing skills developed:*
- Spelling phonetically regular words
- Creating a mental image of words

- Word and sentence dictation
- Proofreading

**Research and evidence-based techniques and strategies embedded in AST-R/S:**
- Sound segmenting
- Sound blending
- Auditory vowel isolation
- Auditory discrimination chains
- Symbol imagery and visualization for spelling
- Mental manipulation of sounds
- Multisyllable processing, segmenting, blending, and dividing rules
- Visualization for comprehension
- Neurological Impress Reading
- Phrasing
- Memory training
- Glass decoding technique
- Davis Reading Correction
- Rehearsed reading
- Neuro-Linguistic Programming spelling strategy
- Strategies Intervention Model (SIM) proofreading strategy: COPS
- Frequency-based auditory training

## Auditory Stimulation and Training–Comprehension (AST-C)

AST- Comprehension is used for students who may be able to read but have challenges with listening and reading comprehension. The sixty directed audio-vocal training lessons specifically address auditory skills needed for good listening and processing of auditory information as well as developing the skills needed for accurate, automatic comprehension.

## *Auditory and comprehension skills developed*

**Getting a clear message:** Accurate discrimination of sounds and syllables, auditory memory, "hearing" the flow and intonation of the language, and attention to detail.

**Visualizing while listening or reading:** People who comprehend well "make a movie" in their head as they read or listen. It is not possible to remember every word that is heard or read, but if the language is stored as images, the content and meaning can be retained and remembered easily.

**Understanding the gestalt** or whole idea of material heard or read and seeing how the details fit into the big picture.

**Understanding the story grammar** or the key content elements in material that is read or heard. This encompasses the who, what, when, where, why, how, problem, and resolution.

**Verbal reasoning:** analyzing and answering inferential and evaluative questions, and verbal problem-solving.

## *Language skills developed*

- Auditory discrimination of similar syllables, phrases, and sentences
- Word order
- Word usage: pronouns, prepositions, articles, verb tense, contractions, plurals, possessives
- Vocabulary

- Intonation
- Fluency
- Flexibility with word order and sentence structure
- Punctuation

*Research/evidence-based techniques and strategies embedded in AST–Comprehension*

- Visualization for comprehension
- Dual coding (integration of visualization and inner verbal language)
- Neurological Impress Reading
- Phrasing
- Memory training
- Listen-Echo-Tap
- Rehearsed reading
- Strategies Intervention Model (SIM) proofreading strategy: COPS
- Frequency-based auditory training
- Rhythm and timing

At seven years old, Sophie had been in speech therapy for nearly two years. She and her mom worked very hard on all of the exercises provided by the speech therapist. Sophie was passing through the grades at school, and it was suggested that she be dismissed from speech, as she had met all of her benchmarks. But functionally, Sophie was not meeting the expectations of her grade level. It was not for lack of trying or intelligence, but the gap between what was expected in school and what Sophie could actually do was widening. She was struggling with reading and comprehension and spending two or more hours each day on homework.

When Sophie spoke, her articulation sounded garbled and had a nasal tone. Later, when her mom learned that Sophie had an auditory processing disorder, she realized that the way Sophie was speaking likely reflected the way her brain was "hearing" language. While Sophie had made progress with her speech therapy, her mom was sure there had to be more to the picture. There was a disconnect between what Sophie could show her and what she intuitively believed her daughter could do.

Sophie was distracted but didn't have ADHD. She had poor, illegible writing. Her mom described her as a couch potato because she had such low energy. Sophie was very shy because she was simply lost in conversation and class and struggled to express herself.

Sophie became a student at Stowell Learning Center doing Auditory Stimulation and Training with an emphasis on comprehension. Stimulated by her sound therapy, Sophie began to develop an awareness of pencil pressure, and her handwriting improved. In fact, she now does beautiful calligraphy. Eye contact and energy increased.

In the fourth month working with AST-Comprehension, Sophie had a breakthrough one night at dinner. She gave a quick response to a question and cracked a joke right behind it! This may sound like a small thing, but to her mom, it was huge. Sophie was beginning to get a clearer message when listening, which allowed her to respond more appropriately and without a delay. Language was becoming more organized and making more sense.

About a year into her training, Sophie decided to try out for a play at school. Her mom tried to talk her out of it, knowing how difficult speaking and expressing herself had always been.

But Sophie's confidence was growing, and she decided to go for it. She got the part and performed beautifully with only one missed line, which she faked! Sophie went on to be the Associated Student Body secretary at school, where the advisor shared that Sophie's notes were the best she'd ever seen.

Auditory processing was the root of Sophie's early challenges. Training the auditory system and building comprehension skills opened Sophie's world to all kinds of possibilities. At her baptism, Sophie, then a junior in high school, spoke confidently and gratefully to the congregation about her journey with auditory processing, school challenges, and the auditory training that opened up her world.

[30] In his book *When Listening Comes Alive* (2015), Paul Madaule discusses the auditory feedback loop and provides exercises for ear-voice training.

[31] Doidge, Norman. *The Brain's Way of Healing: Remarkable Discoveries and Recoveries from the Frontiers of Neuroplasticity.* USA: Penguin Books, 2016, page 295

[32] Shaywitz, Sally. *Overcoming Dyslexia* (2020 Edition): Second Edition, Completely Revised and Updated. 2020, pages 78 - 83. Vintage: (2nd Edition), 2008.

[33] Ron Davis, founder of the Reading Research Counsel, discusses dyslexic confusion with small common sight words in his book *The Gift of Dyslexia* and found that there are 250 of these trigger words (words that trigger confusion and disorientation) that seem to be common among most dyslexic individuals.

[34] Van den Honert, Dorothy. *Wiping out Dyslexia with Enhanced Lateralization: Musings from My Forty Years of Wiping.* AuthorHouse 2012.

Chapter Twenty
## REFLEX INTEGRATION AND MOVEMENT DEVELOPMENT

Learning gets its jumpstart through the involuntary movements caused by the primitive survival reflexes babies are born with or that emerge in the first few months of life. There is a normal progression of movement activity that helps a child understand himself and accurately perceive and navigate his world. Interference, for whatever reason, to this normal development through movement can impact a child's attention, learning, interactions, and comfort in the world. We call these foundational movement patterns and skills Core Learning Skills.

Children with learning and attention challenges are often very inflexible. They are disrupted by any change in routine. They have only one way of doing things because they do not have the physical and mental flexibility to feel secure trying something in a different way. The mental flexibility and adaptability needed for ease in learning, social relationships, and general functioning begin at the Core Learning Skills level. Retraining Core Learning Skills can help learners of any age develop higher brain functions and mental control.

### What are retained or unintegrated reflexes?

Reflexes are automatic movements, or movements that occur without conscious thought. These are programmed into the spinal cord and cannot be controlled by the brain. As humans, we all have them and depend on them throughout life to automatically do the things we need to do. Babies are born with primitive reflexes that help in the birthing process, survival in the first months of life, and the development of visual and motor skills and critical neurological connections for behavior and learning.

As infants grow, reflexes mature and become fully integrated, working in synchrony with the nervous system so we can operate with ease, move smoothly, think clearly, and behave appropriately.

Primitive reflexes will fade into the background, becoming a backup player as needed. For example, the hands-supporting reflex will activate if you fall, causing you to automatically extend your arms and flex your hands to break your fall.

Immature or unintegrated reflexes can place constant stress on the nervous system, as the brain has to work harder to accomplish tasks or behaviors that should be automatic. For example, most daily activities should be performed with relative ease, not requiring a hyper-alert survival state. A retained Moro reflex (the infant startle reflex) can cause a person to operate in a constant state of high alert, causing stress hormones cortisol and adrenaline to be released and weakening the immune system, rational thought, and emotional regulation.

Bonnie Brandes, MEd., developer of QRI (Quantum Reflex Integration therapy), likens reflexes to a symphony.[35] When all are performing properly and in synchrony or integration with the whole, there is harmony and function. If a reflex fails to integrate or assimilate into the nervous system to be used only as needed, there is disharmony, and the ability to choose one's own thoughts, actions, and behaviors will be compromised.

Immature or unintegrated reflexes are often seen in children or adults with sensory processing disorder, attention deficit hyperactivity disorder (ADHD), learning disabilities, and dyslexia, and those on the autism spectrum. Reading and writing difficulties, speech and language delays, disorganization, fidgeting, distractibility, and decreased concentration can all be related to poor reflex integration. Once reflexes are matured and integrated, these children and adults tend to experience greater success and confidence.

### Exercise and Learning

Exercise is a proven stimulus for learning and has become an effective treatment for many disorders. Movement affects energy, attention, mood, memory, and motivation.

A study out of Duke University Medical School showed that physical exercise was equally as successful in decreasing anxiety and depression as medication alone or medication with exercise.

John Ratey, MD, who conducted a study on the effects of exercise on learning with the Naperville School District in Naperville, Illinois, says:

> Exercise increases the concentration of both dopamine and norepinephrine, as well as other brain chemicals. I have always said that a dose of exercise is like taking a bit of Ritalin or Adderall. It's similar to taking a stimulant. Second,

over time, exercise helps build up the machinery to increase the amount of neurotransmitters in the brain as well as their postsynaptic receptors. Chronic exercise eventually causes growth of the system. The more fit that you are, the better the system works.

All students in the Naperville School District participated in a fitness-based PE program for forty minutes daily. Only three percent of their students were found to be overweight as opposed to the 33 percent average in the US at the time. After taking the Trends in International Mathematics and Science Study (TIMSS) as a "country," the Naperville School District ranked number one in the world in science and number six in math. The US typically ranks in the mid-to-low teens.

Studies show that movement is an important factor in brain development. The brain develops by creating neural pathways or connections between different areas of the brain to produce increasingly complex and controlled behavior. Movement increases the levels of glutamate in the brain through BDNF (brain-derived neurotrophic factor). Glutamine is a messenger neurotransmitter that initiates and maintains communication between brain cells.

Movement and exercise stimulate the production of BDNF, small proteins called growth factors involved with modifying the body's vulnerability to stress and supporting memory, learning, and neuroplasticity. "Early on, researchers found that if they sprinkled BDNF onto neurons in a petri dish, the cells automatically sprouted new branches, producing the same structural growth required for learning" (Ratey, 2013). This shows the power of BDNF toward learning, as brain cells need to grow in order to learn anything new.

Exercise activates the prefrontal cortex, our brain's center for focus, self-management, and other executive functions. It readies the brain for learning and turns on attention, memory, and motivation. It helps regulate your emotions and makes your brain better.

### Core Learning Skills Training (CLS)

Core Learning Skills training (CLS) developed by Jill Stowell, MS, involves a series of physical balance and movement activities that improve visual and motor skills, graphomotor (handwriting) skills, internal organization, coordination, self-awareness, self-control, and attention. Exercises are done five days a week to help make neurological connections in the brain that are critical to comfortable learning and functioning. CLS exercises help integrate primitive survival reflexes and improve interpretation of sensory input, physical and mental organization, and learning efficiency.

Core Learning Skills training uses sound therapy and rhythm activities to help the student gain a sense of self as a reference point and an understanding of space and time, which are critical for developing attention, self-control, and organization skills.

In Core Learning Skills training, the aim is not to get the movement "right." We are not training a set of "normal" movements into the child. We are using movements to develop learning.

Learning involves thinking, comparing, evaluating, planning, visualizing, adjusting, and ultimately finding the most effective ways to do things. We are not interested in training in a "splinter" skill that a student can execute but not apply. We are working toward students doing the activities in Core Learning Skills training effortlessly, independently, and with flexibility. If we ask them to start in a different place, use a different foot, try a new pattern, or go at a different speed, they will be willing and able to do so without anxiety if the movements are becoming internalized and automatic. These are the hidden building blocks of learning.

### Core Learning Skills curriculum

Core Learning Skills training consists of eleven core skill areas, each of which has a number of different, sequential activities designed to integrate reflexes, build body awareness and control, increase attention and concentration, and develop visual skills and internal organization needed for learning.

Reflex integration activities provide the cornerstone for the training. CLS training focuses on five reflexes that have a direct impact on skills needed for functioning in the classroom: Moro, Spinal Galant, ATNR, TLR, and STNR. A number of additional reflexes are worked on within CLS activities, including Landau, Head Righting, Hands Grasping, and Babkin Palmomental.

### Learning Reflexes

### Moro reflex

The Moro reflex acts as a baby's primitive fight-or-flight reaction. It is a survival mechanism that helps initiate breathing at birth and which occurs as a reaction to potential danger, such as sudden change of head position, a loud sound, a frightening visual stimulus, or an unpleasant touch.

The baby's Moro reaction is characterized by first taking a deep breath and stretching the arms and legs out away from the body, head back, and then pulling the arms and legs into the middle of the body and starting to cry.

The Moro is fully present at thirty weeks in utero and should be fully integrated after birth by the time the baby is four months old. The Moro reflex is replaced by an adult startle reflex. If it persists in the older child, it can be associated with the following:

- Hypersensitivity
- Hyper-reactivity
- Poor impulse control
- Stimulus-bound effect (cannot ignore peripheral stimuli to focus attention on one thing–has to pay attention to everything)
- Sensory Overload
- Anxiety (particularly anticipation anxiety)
- Volatile emotions
- Temper tantrums
- Emotional and social immaturity
- Poor balance and coordination
- Visual–motor processing problems (inability to fixate, excessive blinking, and difficulty maintaining eye contact)
- Biochemical and nutritional imbalances
- Fatigue and mood swings
- Motion sickness
- Higher incidence of ear and throat infections. When children or adults have a retained Moro, they tend to operate in a heightened state of arousal. This causes intense chemical reactions in the body. The constant secretion of stress hormones such as cortisol and adrenaline puts stress on the immune system, often resulting in allergies and upper respiratory infections and illnesses.

Students with a retained Moro reflex may be seen in the classroom as easily distracted and having difficulty focusing on details, difficulty copying from the board, frequent absences due to allergies and chronic illness, panic attacks, mood swings, anxiety, fearfulness, unexpected changes in behavior, and aggressive outbursts.

### Spinal Galant

The Spinal Galant reflex appears at twenty weeks in utero and integrates between three and nine months of age. When the baby's skin is touched on either side of the spine, the hips will flex towards that side. This reflex helps with the birthing process and allows the fetus to hear and feel vibration in utero by pushing its spine up against the mother's. This is important in the development of auditory processing.

If it is retained beyond nine months, the Spinal Galant can interfere with bladder control, causing bedwetting beyond age five. Children with this reflex often don't like tight-fitting clothing around their waist, and when they have to sit in a chair, they are likely to fidget and squirm and wiggle. It is very difficult to sit still when you have a reflex causing your hips to flex every time you lean against the back of your chair or when your pants are tight around your waist. This reflex is always competing with the child's attention and short-term memory because the child is distracted by the need to be in a constant state of motion.

A retained Spinal Galant reflex affects the following:

- Ability to sit still (fidgety, squirmy, wiggly)
- Attention/concentration
- Short-term memory
- Speech, reading, and spelling

- Coordination
- Gross and fine motor skills
- Posture
- Near focusing
- Bladder control, leading to bedwetting beyond the age of five
- Spine curvature, possibly contributing to the development of scoliosis
- Bowel movements, possibly causing irritable bowel syndrome in adults
- Aversion to clothing that fits tightly around the waist
- Hypersensitivity to touch

In school, students with a retained Spinal Galant reflex may have difficulty with fine motor skills and handwriting, dislike physical education due to coordination difficulties, make noise to relieve pent-up energy, and prefer to do homework lying on the floor. ADHD or ADD, speech disorders, spelling difficulties, auditory processing issues, and poor concentration and short-term memory can be related to a retained Spinal Galant.

### *Asymmetrical Tonic Neck Reflex (ATNR)*

The ATNR in an infant is activated as a result of turning the head to one side. As the head is turned, the arm and leg on the same side will extend while the opposite limbs bend. This pattern helps develop muscle tone and the vestibular system. This reflex is needed at birth so that the fetus can help "unscrew" itself from the birth canal and is the infant's first experience with coordinating both sides of the body together. This is why children born by cesarean section are at a higher risk for developmental delay. Without experiencing this twisting action, they do not get the necessary bilateral integration needed for developing later skills.

The ATNR helps develop hand-eye coordination, as well as visual and auditory processing. Learning difficulties often result from a retained ATNR. The reflex should be inhibited by six months of age.

If the ATNR remains active in a child at a later age, it can affect the following:

- Hand-eye coordination, causing difficulties such as the ability to control the arm and hand when writing, throwing, and catching.
- Binocular vision, the ability for the eyes to work together as a team. Difficulties may result in blurring, double vision, and rubbing and redness of eyes.
- Ability to cross the vertical midline for reading and writing. (A right-handed child may find it hard to write on the left side of the page).
- A discrepancy between oral and written performance (poor handwriting and difficulty expressing ideas on paper); dysgraphia.
- Poor development of lateral eye movements, such as the visual tracking necessary for reading and writing.
- Reading and writing skills, causing dyslexia and problems reading, spelling, and using correct grammar
- Math abilities, causing dyscalculia
- Control of automatic balance; loss of balance and bumping into objects while walking or running
- Bilateral integration (differentiated and integrated use of the two sides of the body)

- Dexterity, for example, the child might drop objects when their head turns
- Attention
- Ability to eat without making a mess
- Ability to be patient, act age appropriately, and share

At school, students with an unintegrated ATNR may experience high distractibility; delayed binocular vision, causing print to "jump around;" omission of letters, words, or whole lines; reversal of letters and numbers; difficulty crossing the midline; difficulty reading small print; spelling and grammar difficulties; dyslexia; poor reading comprehension; impaired handwriting; grip pencil too tightly; writing at an angle across the page; persistence in drawing a circle clockwise and difficulty with writing 8s; unestablished hand, eye, leg, and/or ear dominance; difficulty in following multiple instructions; and poor memory.

### *Symmetric Tonic Neck Reflex (STNR)*

The Symmetrical Tonic Neck Reflex emerges at six to nine months of age and should integrate by nine to eleven months. When the baby is on all fours, bending the legs (sitting on heels), it will cause the head to come up and arms to straighten. When the arms bend, the head will go down, and the bottom will come up as the legs begin to straighten. This rocking motion helps the baby to get on hands and knees in order to crawl and helps develop near to far vision. As the head comes down, his eyes focus to near distance, and as the head is brought back up, the eyes adjust to far distance.

This reflex helps the infant learn to rise on hands and knees in order to creep and crawl. Creeping and crawling are essential for visual development. In fact, creeping is one of the most important movement patterns for helping the eyes move across the midline (vertical centerline) of the body. As the infant moves from one hand to another, the eyes also move from one side to the other. This is very important visual training for reading.

A retained STNR is highly correlated to learning challenges. Without the ability to move the eyes easily across the midline, the child will lose his place often when reading and lose his attention as he crosses the page when writing. The focusing distance from the eyes to the hands and the eye-hand coordination skills used for creeping and crawling are at the same distance that will eventually be used for reading and writing.

If the STNR remains active in an older child, it can affect the following negatively:

- Integration of upper and lower portions of the body (creeping, crawling, and swimming)
- Sitting posture (tendency to slump when sitting at a desk or a table)
- Muscle tone (tone is poorly developed, causing "clumsiness")
- Hand-eye coordination and writing skills
- Attention, concentration, short-term memory
- Visual development (difficulty copying from the board)
- Attention to work (decreasing quality and quantity)
- Ability to read and learn
- Ability to shift focus from near to far and back to near; ability to copy quickly
- Ability to sit and pay attention
- Ability to eat without making a mess

# TAKE THE STONE OUT OF THE SHOE

In the classroom, students with an unintegrated STNR may be seen wrapping their legs around chair legs, sitting on their legs, sitting in a *W* position, fidgeting, or wandering around the classroom. They often have poor impulse control; poor attention and concentration; difficulty changing focus from near to far; reading difficulties, especially while seated; and poor handwriting, short-term memory, and attention to their work.

## *Tonic Labyrinthine Reflex (TLR)*

The TLR is important for developing correct head alignment, balance, visual tracking, auditory processing, and muscle tone.

When the baby's head goes forward, his legs and arms bend and come in toward his body. When the head goes back, the baby's arms and legs straighten. This reflex helps the newborn straighten out at birth and begins to train balance, muscle tone, and proprioception, or the ability to know the position of different body parts.

The TLR forward (flexion) emerges at three to four months in utero and should integrate at approximately three to four months of age. The TLR backward (extension) emerges at birth and integrates at three to four months to three and a half years of age.

If this reflex does not integrate when it should, it gets in the way of developing gravitational security. The child may literally and figuratively feel a little off-balance much of the time because his center of balance is thrown off every time his head moves. He doesn't develop a strong sense of himself as the reference point from which to view the world. He never gets a secure sense of where he is in space, which can affect his sense of direction and understanding of up and down, left and right, and front and back. Interestingly, astronauts in a gravity-free environment (where there is no secure reference point) will show some of the same symptoms that learners with poor reference points do: writing from right to left, reversing letters and numbers, and producing mirror writing.

Characteristics of retained tonic labyrinthine reflex are as follow:

- Weak or tense muscle tone
- Motion sickness
- Difficulty crossing the midline of the body
- Mixed right/left dominance
- Difficulty climbing
- Fatigue, poor stamina
- Poor posture
- Walking late
- Difficulty walking up and down stairs or on uneven ground
- Stiff, jerky movements
- Difficulty judging space, direction, distance, velocity

Students in the classroom with a retained TLR may show difficulty with auditory processing, following verbal directions, blocking out irrelevant signals, reading (comprehension and letter reversals), copying from the board, keeping track of time, and short-term memory. They tend to be disorganized and forgetful; have poor sequencing skills for ordering speech, spelling, composition, and building of concepts; and have poor alignment skills (math columns). Poor language skills, speech disorders, and general lack of alertness are also common.

## Additional Skill Areas

*Rhythm and timing:*

Timing is inherent in everything! Repetitive, rhythmic movement is calming, regulating, and organizing. These activities help improve and internalize rhythm and timing, which ultimately impacts total functioning, including (to name a few) verbal and reading fluency, coordination, social skills, organization, planning, sports, dancing, learning, being on time, and being in sync with the world and others.

*Relaxation and calming:*

Relaxation and calming activities build an awareness of what it feels like to relax, a first step in consciously controlling stress, anxiety, and focus. These activities stimulate the following:

- Proprioception (accurately perceiving information from the joints and limbs)
- Parasympathetic nervous system, which helps pull the person out of fight or flight into a calmer state
- The stapedius muscle in the middle ear, whose job it is to decrease sensitivity to noise
- Ability to rest and refresh the eyes and mind
- Oxygen to the brain, which improves thinking and encourages muscles to relax as they are flooded with oxygen-rich blood
- Ability to reduce anxiety and control stress
- Calmer, clearer state for thinking, learning, emotional balance, and decision-making
- Self-monitoring and control of stress reactions to support clearer thinking for learning, relationships, and problem-solving

*Differentiation and body awareness:*

Individuals with apraxia and challenges with body awareness and control may not be able to locate, isolate, and move specific parts of their body without a great deal of conscious effort or help. This greatly impacts self-control and the ability to coordinate sequences of movements needed for general ease of functioning. For example, throwing a ball involves using the shoulder, elbow, and wrist in a fluent, coordinated sequence. A child who has not differentiated his shoulder, elbow, and wrist may throw with his whole arm in a wild, jerky motion.

*Vestibular stimulation:*

The vestibular system is housed in the inner ear. This is our system of balance and movement. The fluid inside the vestibular organs moves and shifts when the head moves, constantly providing information about the position of the head and body in space (spatial awareness).

The vestibular system allows us to maintain our balance and feel secure that we can move and adjust our movements in space without falling. When the vestibular system is fully functional, we are secure and organized in our bodies and can move calmly, safely, and with confidence and control. The vestibular system helps us prepare our posture, maintain our balance, properly use our vision, calm ourselves, and regulate our behavior.

The constant three-dimensional reference point provided by the vestibular system allows the body to adapt to movement and maintain balance without falling or getting hurt. It coordinates the eyes, head, and body so that the brain can respond to movement through space and body position. It coordinates the two sides of the body. The vestibular system impacts visual processing, coordination of movement, muscle tone, timing, and learning efficiency. It provides information to the brain needed to organize for language, reading, and writing.

*Balance and mind-body control:*

Physical balance is the foundation for attention and mental control. The body must be relaxed and centered to be truly balanced.

Control of balance and attention requires the ability first to keep the eyes focused on and maintain attention on an external object or anchor with eyes open, then internally with eyes closed. Control of balance and attention is more difficult with reduced motion. Balance without movement requires maximum mind-body control. Therefore, arms and body movements should be at a minimum for good mind-body control

*Laterality:*

Laterality is one's internal sense of right and left. In order to be able to functionally understand and use right and left externally in our environment, as with moving to the right or left or discriminating the difference between *b* and *d*, we must first have a sense of right and left on ourselves.

*Midline and bilateral movement:*

The *midline* is the imaginary line running from top to bottom down the center of the body that separates it into right and left halves. Crossing the midline means that one body part (i.e. the hand) is able to go across that center line and work on the other side of the body.

The ability to cross the midline is important for both the body and the brain. The two hemispheres of the brain have different functions and approach tasks from different perspectives. The two hemispheres communicate with each other across the corpus callosum in order to contribute their unique perspective and coordinate movement and learning.

Crossing the midline is developed as children develop bilateral movement skills. Bilateral movement is the ability to use both sides of the body at the same time in controlled, coordinated, organized movement (i.e. writing or cutting with one hand while using the other hand to hold the paper). Students who have poor bilateral coordination may have trouble with basic living skills (tying shoes, getting dressed), fine motor skills (buttoning, stringing beads), visual motor skills (writing, drawing, catching, throwing), and gross motor skills (crawling, walking, climbing stairs, riding a bike).

When a child crosses the midline spontaneously with his dominant hand, that hand will get the practice needed to develop good fine motor skills. If the child avoids crossing the midline, he may tend to use both hands interchangeably to do tasks that should be done with the dominant hand. As a result, both hands get practice, but neither one becomes dominant and expert. Hand dominance does not get firmly established, and fine motor skills, such as pencil control and handwriting, will be affected.

Difficulty crossing the midline may be seen as follows:

- Tips head far to the side and turns the paper or book sideways when writing or reading so that she is never crossing the midline from left to right, but reading or writing essentially from the bottom up.
- Uses one hand on one side of the body and switches

to the other hand at the midline. For example, if a student is pointing under the words as she is reading, she may start out with her left pointer finger and then switch to the right at the midline. Young students sometimes switch the pencil from one hand to another when writing to avoid the midline.

- Shifting the body way over to the left side while writing so they never have to cross the midline.
- Subtle shift of the paper toward the dominant side while writing so the dominant hand never has to reach further than the midline.
- Tend to hold self very stiffly, moving the body as a whole unit instead of turning or rotating their trunk. For example, a student with poor ability to cross the midline may turn his hips or whole body when handing something in his right hand to someone standing to the left of him, as opposed to just turning his upper body.

*Visual skills:*

Visual skills are profoundly important in cognitive development and school success. Visual skills are much, much more than being able to see with 20/20 acuity.

Vision is a complex process involving many different skills. Visual skills, including near-far focusing, eye-hand coordination, eyes following a moving target, integration of vestibular and visual systems, and visualization are developed throughout Core Learning Skills training.

Very specific attention is focused on the development of appropriate response to light, visual tracking, fixation, eye-hand coordination, use of central and peripheral vision, perception of speed and distance, following a moving target, and focusing both eyes together equally and at various distances.

The higher-level skills of visualization, motor planning, and mental flexibility are also developed in the CLS visual activities.

*Graphomotor (handwriting) skills development includes:*
- Reflex integration for reflexes that directly impact handwriting and written expression
- Release exercises that help the student release tension and loosen up the muscles and joints needed for writing
- Alphabet 8s to integrate the movements needed to form letters and increase ability to cross the vertical midline without confusion
- A graphomotor fluency sequence that uses both large and small muscles to increase automaticity and fluency with writing letters
- WriteBrain®, developed by Jeannette Farmer, to increase integration, impulse control, attention, and writing fluency

*Aerobics:*
Research has shown that aerobic exercise is highly effective in decreasing hyperactivity and increasing memory, attention, concentration, mood, and thinking. Aerobic activity increases blood flow and oxygen to the brain and is valuable to people of all ages for general health and well-being.

### Quantum Reflex Integration (QRI)

Quantum Reflex Integration (QRI)[36] combines low-intensity laser (light), sound, and reflex integration techniques to stimulate the nervous system and repattern both primitive and lifelong reflexes. A child's development may not progress smoothly until all the reflexes are integrated and working together.

QRI has been a valuable tool for helping our students with various learning or attention challenges, including dyslexia, auditory processing, attention deficits, autism spectrum, executive function, learning disabilities, and processing skills.

If you think of the nervous system like a highway with messages between the brain and body traveling on it, unintegrated reflexes are like roadblocks. Humans are survivors and find ways to work around difficulties and even neurological roadblocks, but workarounds and compensations are typically less efficient and cause a delay, resulting in the person always being a little behind in real time.

QRI acts to repair the roadblocks for more fluent, efficient functioning and learning. While we can't physically *see* the strengthened neurological connections stimulated by QRI in our students, we have seen the following:

- Non-verbal students start to speak
- High-anxiety students become settled and available for learning
- Rational thinking and problem-solving improve
- Greater body awareness and control
- Improved emotional regulation and motivation
- Improved attention
- Increased self-awareness and overall calm

QRI is a highly effective tool for integrating reflexes and improving neural connections for learning and functioning because, applying the principle of neuroplasticity, it stimulates and repatterns reflex pathways.

## The science of light and color[37]

The therapeutic use of light has a very long history. The ancient Egyptians knew that sunlight could promote healing and growth, and second-century Romans and Greeks used sunlight as a treatment for depression. In 1903, a Danish physician, Neil Finsen, won the Nobel prize for his pioneering work with light therapy to treat smallpox.

The optic nerve responds to light as a part of the system of sight, but light also turns on chemical reactions in living organisms that help regulate our biological clock, major organ systems, appetites, hormones, levels of arousal, and the nervous system. The individual cells and proteins in the body have extraordinary sensitivity to color, and because different colors have different wavelengths and frequencies, they stimulate different effects.

## The physics of lasers

Every atom has a nucleus with electrons orbiting around it. When the electrons are close to the nucleus, they have lower energy. If they are farther from the nucleus, they have higher energy and are said to be in an excited state. Most of the time, the electrons in atoms are in low-energy inner orbits. By bombarding atoms with an outside energy source (such as a laser), we can create atoms with an excited, high-energy state. Now there is a higher population of higher-energy electrons than lower. This is called *population inversion*.

Lasers artificially stimulate or bombard atoms to bring about population inversion. This leads to a large release of photons, which in turn stimulate nearby atoms.

When photons are absorbed by living tissue, they stimulate chemical reactions in the light-sensitive molecules in the tissue.

Different molecules absorb different wavelengths of light. Humans have four kinds of photo-sensitive cells, allowing light to be absorbed for vision, in the red blood cells, in muscle, and in all cells. This is the reason lasers are so effective for healing so many conditions. Mitochondria, the cellular power station in cells, is surrounded by a thin layer of light-sensitive cytochrome molecules.

As the sun's photons pass through that membrane, they are absorbed by the light-sensitive cytochrome and stimulate the production of ATP (adenosine triphosphate) molecules that store energy in our cells–like an all-purpose battery.

### Low-intensity laser

QRI uses a low-intensity, or low-level, laser. Low-level laser therapy works by helping the body use its own energy and its own cellular resources to heal itself and strengthen neural pathways with no side effects.

Low-intensity laser therapy is based in the scientific literature of more than three thousand publications and more than two hundred clinical trials with positive results.

### QRI sessions

When QRI is prescribed for students at the Learning Center, they generally do 1.5 hours per week spread into one, two, or three sessions. This is a passive therapy, so the student lies on a massage table, generally on their back, while the clinician places and moves the lasers through the prescribed patterns. The laser is not hot, and it is either laid on the student on certain points or moved in specific patterns about an inch off the body. QRI tends to be very relaxing for students, so they usually close their eyes and often fall asleep.

In fact, when hyper-vigilant students relax enough to close their eyes and eventually fall asleep, we know they have made a real breakthrough.

QRI has an extensive reflex integration protocol and a number of prescriptive and specialty protocols. We look very specifically at each student's functional needs and retained reflexes in order to create target goals and protocols for their QRI therapy.

### QRI Outcomes with ADHD

Shannon was almost six when she started QRI. She had been diagnosed with ADHD, and while extremely bright and doing well academically in school, she was disruptive to everyone around her and constantly in trouble at school. She was overly touchy and aggressive with others, had very high energy, and was extremely impulsive and distractible. She had trouble getting work done due to poor attention and resistant behavior. She showed subtle problems with speech and had to concentrate hard on what she wanted to say. Her parents had to repeat themselves many times when asking her to do something.

Shannon did a nine-week protocol of QRI. Unlike most of our students, whose programming involves a number of programs and strategies, Shannon was doing QRI only.

In her initial few sessions, she was very chatty and social but very impulsive and strong-willed. She constantly grabbed at things and deliberately disobeyed, but was coy about it, watching to see if she was getting a reaction. She was very wiggly. Her legs were fidgety at the beginning of each reflex pattern, and then she would settle very briefly. She was not able to sustain for the repetitions and would pop up and start flitting around the room, picking up things at random and chattering. She could not sustain through the full thirty-minute session.

Shannon did two sessions a week. Weeks one through four were rough both at home and school. Her dad was very concerned. He felt that in the four weeks of QRI, Shannon had been much more defiant and that her attention problems had escalated. Her mom met with her teacher, who also indicated that Shannon had been much more difficult and defiant in the previous three weeks.

Shannon's mom noticed that Shannon's eyes seemed dilated (an indication of a reactive Moro reflex). Shannon told her teacher, "My bones are not controlled. It's my bones doing it, not me." She told her mom that she felt out of control.

Shannon had a very strong Moro, and we felt that we were witnessing Moro reorganization. The fact that she could verbalize that she felt out of control indicated an important increase in self-awareness.

Things started to turn around for Shannon at week six. She had a good week at school with only one minor incident and had a good weekend as well.

Week eight, Shannon's mom felt that things were improving, and Dad had not voiced any concerns in two weeks. There were no notable challenges at school, daycare, or over the weekend.

Mom felt Shannon seemed forgetful, which she had never been before. She said, "I tell her something, and she immediately forgets it."

At the Learning Center, we felt that Shannon's physical hyperactivity had dramatically decreased but that her mind was still very busy. When she was physically all over the place, her mom had to get her attention before telling her something. Once Shannon's body was calmer, her mom was just telling her without getting her attention first, so Shannon, absorbed in whatever she was doing or thinking, did not register what Mom said.

Week nine brought a dramatic improvement in Shannon's calmness and compliance. She came in for her QRI session quietly and followed all directions. She put her toys down when asked and was polite and appropriate when speaking.

We discussed "Stop and Think" and trying to use it at school, which, at her next session, she reported that she did. She explained that her friend had apples and peanut butter and she wanted some, so she kept saying to her friend, "Share your food; share your food." She then told herself, "Stop and Think," and stopped telling her friend to share. This was a big step for Shannon in conscious management of her behavior and impulse control.

We opted to continue with QRI sessions, but here is what Shannon's mom said after her initial nine-week protocol.

"We are so thrilled with the results of QRI. Shannon is doing great! The last three weeks have been amazing. She is calm. She's not impulsive. She's telling the truth now. It's almost scary good because it's so not like her! Her aunt and cousin, who aren't aware that we are doing QRI, noticed over the weekend that Shannon was so quiet and well-behaved. The week before spring break, Shannon's teacher said, 'Oh my gosh, she's an exemplary student!' That's just so amazing to hear from a teacher!"

[35] Brandes, Bonnie, MEd. *The Symphony of Reflexes: Interventions for Human Development, Autism, ADHD, CP, and Other Neurological Disorders.* Create Space, 2015.

[36] QRI was developed by Bonnie Brandes. Information about QRI training, products, and success stories can be found at www.reflexintegration.net.

[37] The science of light and laser for rewiring neural circuits is discussed in *The Brain's Way of Healing: Remarkable Discoveries and Recoveries from the Frontiers of Neuroplasticity*, Chapter 4, by Norman Doidge, MD

Chapter Twenty One
## COGNITIVE PROCESSING SKILLS TRAINING

Research indicates that brain training can change cognitive functioning based on the concepts of neuroplasticity and external stimulation. The key skills developed in this type of training are working memory, processing speed, attention, mental flexibility, problem-solving, and reasoning. These skills are needed for quickly acquiring, assimilating, retaining, and responding to information—in other words, for thinking and learning.

Cognitive training activities are not academic—they do not look like school—but as these foundational processing skills improve, the student's ability to take in and retain academic instruction also increases.

*Intensity and making errors* Intensity is a critical factor in cognitive skills training. The things that push us the most are the things that will create the most change. Making errors is important in learning and neuroplasticity because as errors are made, the brain makes micro-adjustments to figure it out. We do cognitive training activities with our students, in short, intense bursts working at a challenging level so the the brain has the increasing opportunity to learn through recognizing, making, and correcting errors. At the same time, the beat of the metronome is regulating and repetitive, which pushes the learning to a more automatic level and becomes calming to the nervous system.

Dr. Andrew Huberman, neuroscientist and professor of ophthalmology and neurobiology at Stanford School of Medicine, says:

> "The way to create plasticity is to send signals to the brain that something is wrong, something is different, and something isn't being achieved. Flow is an expression of what we already know how to do–it is not a state for learning. Errors and making errors out of sync with what we would like to do is how our nervous system is cued through very distinct biological mechanisms that something isn't going right and therefore certain neurochemicals are deployed that certain neurocircuits have to change."[38]

### Feedback

Cognitive training is most effective when provided on a one-to-one basis so that the student can be given specific, immediate feedback. Some struggling students are so used to making mistakes that they start guessing at random as soon as they read the instructor or parent's face and know that whatever they did was incorrect. Specific feedback helps students to recognize what parts they did correctly and exactly what the errors were. Studies indicate that immediate feedback is far more effective in improving performance than delayed feedback.

### Regulation

A metronome has many benefits in cognitive training. Adding the metronome to an activity increases the intensity, heightens alertness, and helps improve sustained attention and response speed. At the same time, the beat of the metronome is regulating and repetitive, which pushes the learning to a more automatic level and becomes calming to the nervous system.

## *Attention*

There are four types of attention[39] trained in cognitive skills training:

- **Sustained attention**: the ability to maintain attention and consistency of performance over time. At the highest level, sustained attention involves holding and manipulating information in working memory.

- **Selective attention**: the ability to maintain focus in the presence of internal or external distractions; for example, blocking out classroom noise while working on an independent assignment.

- **Alternating attention**: the ability to mentally shift one's attention. This is the mental flexibility that allows a person to shift their attention from one kind of activity or task to another with different expectations in terms of behavior or response.

- **Divided attention**: the ability to respond to two or more things at one time as in listening to the teacher, mentally organizing the information, and taking notes.

## Increasing neuroplasticity through focus

Neuroplasticity requires mental focus. Our eyes provide us a built-in mechanism to increase focus, as focus in the brain is anchored to visual focus.[40] The pupils of the eye have the most visual receptors, so acuity will be much stronger in the center of our vision than in our peripheral vision.

When your eyes are relaxed and moving through space, you have an expanded visual field. Moving the eyes slightly inward narrows the visual field and increases focus.

If you are having trouble absorbing something that you are studying or reading, chances are your eyes are moving around or you're picking up visual input from the environment around you. Practicing narrowing your visual field will help train the brain to focus.

Many cognitive training exercises give students the opportunity to practice visual focus.

## Attention, Memory, and Processing Skills (AMPS)

AMPS[41] is a cognitive processing skills program based on proven ideas from the fields of behavioral optometry and cognitive neuroscience. It was developed by Dr. Douglas Stephey. The brain exercises in AMPS are designed to improve mental processing speed, working memory, attention, sequential processing, spatial orientation, visual and auditory memory, phonological awareness, visual perceptual and tracking skills, motor planning, problem-solving, and reasoning.

Activities are highly varied, fun, and done with intensity. AMPS utilizes games, manipulatives, physical movement activities, and drills that are timed or done with a metronome. Students work on a variety of types of activities within each session.

AMPS training is provided on a one-to-one basis with students either onsite or remotely for a minimum of one hour daily, four days a week. This program is also highly effective when done intensively for two hours a day, five days a week, over a period of seven weeks.

### Processing and Cognitive Enhancement (PACE)

This is a cognitive training program that improves processing skills needed for easy, independent learning and functioning. Skills trained include attention, memory, processing speed, auditory and visual processing, and logic and reasoning.

The PACE program[42] has a very robust and comprehensive phonemic awareness component that builds the student's ability to think about the sounds in syllables containing one to five sounds. These auditory activities focus on discriminating, blending, segmenting, manipulating, reading, and spelling sounds that are heard or seen.

Students work one-to-one with a trainer four to six hours per week doing a variety of procedures in each session for approximately seventy-two hours. Activities are fun and challenging. Intensity and concentration are built through the use of the metronome for the majority of the activities. Reasoning skills and mental flexibility are strongly embedded into the program as procedure levels increase in difficulty and complexity.

PACE was developed by Dr. Ken Gibson, founder of Learning Rx. It has been highly effective in improving phonemic awareness, visual processing skills, attention, executive function, and overall learning efficiency with our students.

### Attention Process Training (APT)

APT[43] is a cognitive training approach that helps reorganize brain systems for more efficient thinking and learning. It is provided on a one-to-one basis three or more times each week for thirty to ninety minutes for a total of approximately forty-eight hours.

Students work with a variety of sequenced activities that train working memory and the attention components critical to new learning: sustained attention, selective attention, alternating attention, and divided attention. One to two types of attention are worked on in each session.

The student and trainer dialogue about what type of attention they are working on, what the student noticed about his attention while doing the activity, and what adjustments he will try in order to increase his performance. Students are also coached to notice their attention outside of sessions, and goals are set to intentionally apply new skills and strategies.

### Perception Attention Therapy (PATH Therapy)

PATH Therapy was developed by neurobiologist Dr. Teri Lawton to help improve neuro-timing, attention span and stamina, visual perception for reading, memory, and processing speed. This unique computer-based cognitive training program focuses on retraining the two visual pathways in the brain to work together optimally. PATH permanently improves the timing in the brain so that the mind is able to focus on the letters in words and the words on the page, allowing the student to take in and decode the information accurately. This program is particularly effective in addressing problems with disorientation and attention loss when reading, and reading fluency, stamina, and comprehension.

Students generally do PATH twice a week. PATH requires intense concentration and visual focus, so sessions are limited to twenty minutes. We typically have the student do a timed reading before each PATH session so that together, we can track changes in reading speed and accuracy.

After each PATH session, we have the student read a one-page passage three times, working to increase speed and accuracy with each reading.

Because PATH Therapy is working at the brainstem level of neuro-timing, we have also found it to be an effective tool for achieving overall improvements in regulation and attention.

[38] Huberman, Andrew. Huberman Lab Podcast Episode 7, "How to Learn Faster by Using Failure, Movement and Balance," Feb. 15, 2021.

[39] *APT-II Attention Process Training* by Sohlberg, Johnson, Paule, Raskin, and Mateer provides information and training activities for the 4 types of attention.

[40] Huberman, Andrew. Huberman Lab Podcast Episode 24, "Science of Vision and Eye Health," June 14, 2021

[41] AMPS was developed by developmental optometrist Dr. Douglas Stephey. Trainer certification is available through Stowell Training Services, Inc. www.learning100.com

[42] PACE was researched and developed by Dr. Ken Gibson and LearningRx. Provider certification training is available through LearningRx: www.pacelearningskills.com.

[43] The Attention Process Training Programs (APT) by Sohlberg and Mateer are based on extensive neurorehabilitation research widely published in the cognitive rehabilitation and traumatic brain injury and neurorehabilitation literature. APT programs are published by Lash and Associates.

Chapter Twenty Two
# PRINCIPLES FOR ENHANCING ATTENTION, BEHAVIOR, AND EXECUTIVE FUNCTION

Much of what we do on a day-to-day, moment-to-moment basis is habit driven, but when it's not, executive function is generally involved. Executive function allows us to self-monitor and manage our own attention and behavior. These are real-life problem-solving, planning, and decision-making skills that need to be developed in real life and real time. Research in neuroscience has shown that people build thinking skills little by little over time as they practice them in the actual situations that are causing the difficulty.[44] As parents or teachers help children consistently practice the following principles, both the child and adult guide become more flexible and make changes in their executive function.

## A Shift in Perspective
### Continuum of arousal

In the neuroscience world, attention and stress are looked at as a continuum of arousal. At the highest level of the continuum, we're so stressed that we're in survival mode–fight, flight, freeze, or fib. At the lowest level, the person is "zonked."

The ideal place for learning and rational thought is in the middle–the "Zone"–where the person has calm, focused alertness.

Emotional regulation and self-management depend upon a level of arousal that is closer to the Zone than either end of the continuum. If we want to help children learn, behave differently, pay attention, or problem-solve, it's not going to happen while operating at either end of that arousal continuum. We have to be aware and help our children and students be aware of where their arousal level is and how to either increase or decrease it. As we work with students on changing their behavior, improving their attention, or building specific executive function skills or habits, we can really only do that effectively if the student is in the Zone or close to it. If they're in fight or flight, it won't work. If they're exhausted, they're not mentally available.

### What does the behavior really mean?

No matter what it looks like, behavior always means something. If behavior needs to be changed, we have to first identify the real root of the problem. What we have to ask as parents and clinicians is, "What is this behavior telling me?"

All behavior serves us in some way. This doesn't mean that the behavior is manipulative; it just means that our behavior reflects a need that we have. It may be a symptom of lagging skills–the person simply doesn't have the needed skills to do what is expected, so they procrastinate, resist, change the subject, or avoid doing what is asked in any number of ways.

Maybe the person is overwhelmed or on sensory overload. Their arousal level is too high, so their survival mechanisms kick in. These survival mechanisms usually show up in some form of fight, flight, freeze, or fib. So we have the child who lashes out (fight), runs (flight), goes blank on a test or hides out in the restroom (freeze), or lies about having homework (fib). The question is, "How is that behavior serving the student, and what is at the real root of the problem?" The student didn't go blank on the test because he wanted to fail. Perhaps this is a student who has comprehension challenges, so in spite of studying relentlessly before a test, he gets extreme anxiety because he knows he doesn't understand the material. Going blank allows him an out and is a better excuse for a poor grade than being dumb or trying hard and failing anyway.

The student who tunes out or daydreams in class may have an auditory processing or comprehension problem. The student may be in a growth spurt or too busy and, therefore, perpetually tired. The student may have a creative thinking style that takes flight when information is boring, difficult, or simply triggers a series of thoughts.

### Building executive function takes practice

Executive function develops all the way through childhood, but the bulk of the development coincides with the major growth in the frontal lobe starting at about eleven or twelve years of age and continuing through about age twenty-five.

When children are very young, direction and decision-making will need to come mainly from the key adults in their lives. But as they grow, children and teens need the opportunity to exercise their executive function.

When parents and teachers, however well-meaning, micromanage or direct every piece of a child's life or make the child pay attention, behave, or comply, they may be inadvertently taking away the child's opportunity to exercise and practice using their own developing executive function skills.

On a busy morning, a mom might say to her son before school, "Go get your backpack and soccer bag and get in the car. You have soccer practice after school at 3:30, and it takes twenty minutes to get there, so come straight to the front of the school after class, or you'll be late to practice, and you know how upset your coach gets when kids are late."

Mom is most likely seeing a mental movie of everything that has to happen before and after school because that's what our executive function does when planning, but notice it was her executive function that got exercised here.

It takes a little bit more time, but instead of telling her son everything that is going to happen and everything he needs to do, guiding him through questioning will stimulate his ability to plan and organize in time and space. She might say, "What do you have after school today?" Now the student has to visualize the calendar and his day. "Oh, it's Tuesday. I have soccer right after school at 3:30."

Then Mom might ask, "What's your plan for getting there on time with your equipment?" giving her son the opportunity to think about time and what he needs. "I get out of class at 3:00, and it takes twenty minutes to get to the field. Can you pick me up right at 3:00 so I'm not late? I'd better put my soccer bag in the car now because there won't be time to come home and get it." Planning requires visualizing and thinking about the future.

Kids need the opportunity and guidance to practice this kind of mental planning and problem-solving throughout their day. They should be given clear directives and then allowed a moment to process and respond. If the student can't work it out and follow the directive on their own, problem-solving together provides a skill-building opportunity.

# TAKE THE STONE OUT OF THE SHOE

## Problem Solve Together[45]

*Step #1 What does the student need?*

Observe, explore, dialogue, and listen to understand what is really beneath the behaviors you are seeing. What does your child/student need? Ask and listen without judgment. Don't share your opinion or give advice. You might lead the discussion with, "I notice . . . Tell me about that."

For example: Your teen does her homework but consistently forgets to turn it in. Try saying, "I notice that you have a lot of missing homework assignments. Tell me about that." There's a good chance your child will say, "I don't know. I just forgot."

Now it's time to explore. "Do you get to class on time? What happens when you get to class—are you early, or do you feel rushed?"

Maybe you discover that between classes is the only time your daughter can talk to friends, so when she gets to class, she doesn't have time to find her homework in her backpack before class starts. Now we know that this student needs time to talk to friends, that it's important to her. We also know that she doesn't have a good organizational system for quickly finding and retrieving her homework.

Students who struggle with behavior, attention, or executive function are continually told how they should behave. Assumptions are made about their motives and abilities. STOP! Take this time to listen and understand what the student needs in order to be successful.

*Step #2 What change is needed?*

Share with the student what you need, what is needed in the classroom, or what change is needed. Be clear. Do not blame. Do not tell the student what to do. For example, with our student who does her work but forgets to turn it in: Homework has to be turned in on time. It is her job as a student and your expectation as her parent.

### Step #3 Collaborate on a solution

Now that the needs on both sides of the problem are understood, together, brainstorm all of the possible solutions —no idea is too crazy. I like to have a big whiteboard where we can write down all of the options. Here are some possible solutions for our student who doesn't turn in her homework:

- Don't do the homework
- Don't talk to friends in passing period
- Put the homework for each class in the textbook for that class
- Have a bright red homework folder that she can easily see in her backpack
- Set the timer on her phone each passing period and get to class a minute earlier.

Together, evaluate each option. Have the student visualize and talk through each solution in order to determine the best solution or strategy to meet both needs. Here's how that might look for our solutions above:

- The student visualizes her parents' reactions to her not doing her homework. She can imagine that her parents will be upset and she will probably not be allowed to see her friends on the weekend. Hmmm. Not good. When she visualizes how that will look at school, she feels like a slacker because she didn't even try to do her homework. She eliminates that option.

- Option number two does not meet both needs, and she can picture how bad she will feel when her friends think she's mad at them because she's not talking to them in the halls. This option gets eliminated as well.

Each option should be visualized and given consideration. Rationale for accepting or rejecting the solution should be verbalized.

Once a solution is decided upon, everyone involved needs to commit to trying it for a short, given amount of time. Then, at the end of the trial period (day or week), evaluate together how it worked, make any needed modifications, and go for it again.

This kind of joint problem-solving takes time but is time well spent. It allows the student to repeatedly practice the very essence of what executive function does. Our executive functions evaluate a situation; determine that there is a problem and what it is; look at multiple perspectives and solutions; determine the best course of action; organize and sequence the steps in the strategy or solution; execute; evaluate; and modify as needed.

### The Dopamine Reward

Dopamine[46] is a brain chemical that increases energy, motivation, and our internal sense of well-being. When dopamine is released, epinephrine (the same chemical as adrenaline, but called epinephrine in the brain) also tends to be released. Epinephrine is involved with increasing a sense of agitation, urgency, and desire and willingness to go, to move forward.

Dopamine is released when something good happens. It is also released in anticipation of things. Anytime we are focused on an external goal, dopamine is cued up, anticipating a milestone, and keeps you moving forward toward it. Each time a milestone or goal is reached, the brain gets another dopamine reward. As applied to executive function, behavior, or attention training, having realistic goals and small, manageable steps helps trigger the dopamine reward system, which helps increase energy, motivation, sense of urgency, willingness to move forward, and sense of accomplishment.

### Inner Language

Think about your week. What's going on this week? What appointments do you have? What do you really want to make sure you have time for? I'll bet you looked up and pictured your calendar and maybe did a little self-talk to answer these questions.

Planning, problem-solving, and organizing require mental forethought—thinking into the future in time and space and mentally manipulating the pieces of the puzzle. We do this through our inner language.

There are two types of inner language: visual inner language or visualization, and verbal inner language or talking ourselves through things.

Visualization is the ability to create mental images. At a basic level, this is visual memory, the ability to mentally picture something we have seen. At the highest level, this is the ability to create and manipulate mental images of thoughts or ideas. Comprehension depends on the ability to turn language into mental images.

Visualization is a key factor in executive functions such as planning, organizing, problem-solving, and seeing multiple perspectives and solutions. It has an important role in mental flexibility, allowing us to create a mental picture and change it as more information is received, or visualize and compare different options.

The mind reasons through verbalization. Language gives us a tool for evaluating actions before they happen and helps curb impulsiveness. We want to teach children to use their inner language to question and guide themselves in order to bring executive function to a conscious level.

Nicholas was fourteen years old and in eighth grade when he came to the learning center. He was a twice exceptional student, being both gifted and having attention and learning challenges. Nicholas was constantly in trouble at school because he operated completely without forethought. He would walk past someone and knock all the papers off their desk. When the other student got upset, he would say, "I didn't mean to!" Of course the other student would protest, "I just watched you do it!"

We asked Nicholas if he ever thought about what he was going to do before he did it. Did he make a plan? His response was, "I like to live in the present." He couldn't visualize potential consequences to his behavior and would impulsively do things as an "experiment." The papers were there; he wanted to see what they would look like falling from the desk.

We started working with Nicholas on visualizing himself doing things before he did them and predicting what would happen. We applied this to every single thing we did, every place we went, everyone he talked to in the center. Before long, he started to control his impulses, and even more, he started to be able to take perspective and predict how others would react if he were to do something.

## Metacognition

Metacognition is using your verbal inner language to do the following:

- Think about your own thinking
- Be consciously aware of your own problem-solving
- Monitor, plan, and control your own mental processing
- Accurately judge your own level of learning

It's like standing on the outside looking in on what your brain is doing. And it dramatically affects school, life, and social success.

As we work with students to develop executive function, we want to talk to them about consciously being aware of their thinking. Encourage them to notice and then share how they were thinking when they decided what kind of pizza to choose or what video game to play. When doing their homework, how do they decide what assignment to do first? What do they say to themselves?

Regularly ask metacognitive questions during the day. Then begin to ask students what questions they should be asking themselves. For example, if there is a test coming up, you might ask the following:

- What strategies will you use to study for your test?
- What has worked well for you in the past?

After the test, ask the following:

- How did you do?
- Did you do as well as you thought?

- What do you think worked for you?
- What will you change for next time?

This kind of thinking about our thinking does not automatically happen for many students, so we need to teach students a problem-solving strategy and help them apply it over and over again as problems come up until it becomes engrained in their thinking:

- What is the problem?
- What is my plan?
- Am I following my plan?
- Is it working?/How did it work?
- How should I adjust my plan?/What should I change for next time?

Metacognition allows students to stand back and evaluate their responses and actions so they can consciously change their behavior or make better choices. Students with ADHD tend to be impulsive, reacting first and thinking later. They may be moving so fast physically or mentally that they don't have time to register feedback. As a result, they may be unaware that they are failing a course, have not started a project on time, or have inadvertently hurt someone's feelings.

Researchers at the Mount Sinai School of Medicine found improvement in ADHD symptoms in adults who participated in metacognitive therapy.[47]

## Build the Critical Underlying Skills

The best guidance and strategies in the world will not work if the student does not have the skills to do the job. For example, a student with auditory processing disorder may have spotty, disorganized lecture notes. Teaching the student a note-taking strategy will not fix this problem. The problem is that the student is working excessively hard to get the information when listening and quite possibly reading the teacher's lips. The information is coming in too fast for her delayed auditory system to process, so there are gaps, and she is constantly trying to connect the dots. There is no mental attention left to think about the note-taking strategy, and as soon as the student looks down at her paper, she has lost the critical visual input of the teacher's mouth and body language.

The first step in the solution for this student is not a note-taking strategy, but auditory training so she can get good input to think with. Then she has both the mental energy and the information to apply to new note-taking skills.

[44] Ablon, Stuart. *Changeable: How Collaborative Problem Solving Changes Lives at Home, at School, and at Work.* TarcherPerigee, 2018, pg. xix

[45] Adapted from the Collaborative Problem Solving Approach developed by Dr. Stuart Ablon, director of Think:Kids in the Department of Psychiatry at Massachusetts General Hospital.

[46] Dopamine is a fascinating chemical. Two excellent resources to learn more: Huberman, Andrew. Huberman Lab Podcast Episode 12, "Increase Motivation and Drive," Mar. 22, 2021

Leiberman, Daniel and Long, Michael. *The Molecule of More: How a Single Chemical in Your Brain Drives Love, Sex, and Creativity and Will Determine the Fate of the Human Race.* BenBella Books, 2018.

[47] The Mount Sinai Hospital/Mount Sinai School of Medicine. "Meta-cognitive therapy more effective for adult ADHD patients." ScienceDaily. ScienceDaily, 1 April 2010.

Chapter Twenty Three
## PUTTING IT ALL TOGETHER

Hamid was a first-year medical student. Well, let's put it this way: he failed his first year of medical school. He was obviously bright and motivated, but the learning challenges that he had successfully worked around all the way through his undergrad premed studies caught up with him with the rigors of medical school.

When we tested Hamid at Stowell Learning Center, we found that he had dyslexia and inefficient processing skills. Hamid did an intensive eight-week program of PACE and AST-Reading and Spelling, attending sessions three hours per day to improve his overall processing skills and correct his dyslexic challenges. He successfully resumed his medical school training the following semester.

Steve was in ninth grade when his school sent him to Stowell Learning Center. Steve had been expelled for pulling a pocket knife at school. Steve was receiving special education services because he had extremely low academic skills and had expressive and receptive language delays.

Steve was being bullied at school. He tried to get help from a teacher at school, but his language skills were so poor that neither the situation nor his distress were understood. So he decided he had to be prepared to defend himself–hence the knife that got him kicked out of school.

When Steve started with us he was extremely withdrawn and noncommunicative, and the first few weeks were like pulling teeth to get any engagement at all. I'm sorry for the circumstances that brought Steve to us, but having the opportunity to really dig into the underlying neurodevelopmental, auditory, language, reading, writing, and comprehension skills at the Learning Center changed his life. He has given me permission to share his story in his own words. What an amazing kid, and what a transformation!

Here's a letter Steve wrote to me when he finished at the Learning Center:

When I first attended here in early 2015, I was anxious. I was very nervous. I had not been in school since September of 2014. Throughout the first months, I learned PACE, rebuilt my math skills and foundations, and AST Comprehension. For math, back in middle school through early high school, I did not even try doing any of the math homework. I felt as if I could not do it and lacked motivation. Once I came over to Stowell they proceeded to teach me the very basics of math, to build a foundation then onward toward higher grade math. I felt much more confident in math. I had a feeling of "Wow, I can actually do this," and my motivation for math grew.

With AST Comprehension, it helped me slow down with reading since I was basically Speedy McGee, which did not help at all with remembering the story, such as main points, the plot, why this character did this or that, etc. AST Comprehension also helped me in reading more fluently and making pictures in my head to better help me remember the story.

PACE I found fun and interesting. It is essentially brain games to train your mind and challenge it. With PACE, it helped me to focus, think quicker, and solve problems and puzzles as quickly as possible. With each level getting more challenging and interesting, surely it benefited me.

After the summer of 2015, my programs changed since I was going back to school, but the school was not just an ordinary one; it was a middle college. My new school assigned more homework than a regular school, so my programs at Stowell helped me more on doing my homework and organization, which is executive function and QRI (Quantum Reflex Integration). These programs started to play a beneficial role for me. I have always had pretty bad anxiety that made it so much harder for me to focus in school and have a social life. It was very limiting for me. QRI relaxes your body as well as integrates your reflexes, which helps in learning and being more focused in a learning environment. QRI reduced my anxiety and helped in learning. Executive function helped me in visualizing which homework to do and helped with my organization skills.

The clinicians were very helpful and motivated toward helping me turn in my homework and step up my game plan for this school year. I was assigned to read two books on a career I may be interested in. I chose Life Coaching, since I enjoy helping people who need it, such as in their job, events, and situations in life that affect them, etc. The two books were over three hundred pages long, and with the foundation AST Comprehension provided, it helped me on better visualizing and remembering what I read and understanding the points so much more.

I can really say that without Stowell, I would not be as focused, motivated, confident, and comfortable to be back in school. They have truly helped me, and I cannot describe how thankful I am to have had the chance for them to help me grow in life and at school. The clinicians made me feel comfortable here, and they became sort of like older siblings that you could connect with and help you, in my opinion. I will always remember my time being here, the memories of creating spirit weeks for all of the students attending Stowell, setting up a field trip, laughing, learning, thinking about my future more, and much, much more. I am honored to have attended here, and it has been an experience that I shall always be glad for. I truly would not be the better me I am today without the Stowell family!

Sincerely,
Steve Lopez

Chapter Twenty-Four
# IT'S TIME TO TAKE THE STONE OUT OF THE SHOE

The world is full of children and adults who used to have a learning problem. I like to think that I have had something to do with that, along with the incredible team at Stowell Learning Centers and colleagues around the world who simply couldn't be satisfied with putting a Band-Aid on a correctable learning challenge.

The brain science, the clinical evidence, and the tools are available to help struggling students put their struggles behind them.

It is no longer acceptable to assume that compensations, workarounds, accommodations, or lesser options are the only choices for the 20–30 percent of students in every school who struggle to achieve their potential.

It's possible and well past time to time to take the stone out of the shoe!

JILL STOWELL

*Acknowledgements*

I am deeply grateful for all of the teachers, researchers, therapists, program developers, and parents who are working so diligently to understand and help struggling students and neurodivergent learners. Their work has provided the basis for the Learning Skills Continuum Approach, programs that address the root of learning challenges, and the practical tools for supporting struggling learners that you will find in this book.

In particular, I want to acknowledge Dr. Joan Smith, my mentor and friend who challenges my thinking and whose influence is evident everywhere in this book and in my work.

Also of tremendous influence is Alex Doman, whose work in the field of sound and auditory training has had a profound impact on our students and our ability to truly change the future for students with various learning challenges.

In April of 2020, when the world locked down due to the COVID-19 pandemic, we decided to support parents and teachers through a livestream broadcast, LD Expert Live. I have to thank our incredible LD Expert Live team: my husband, David Stowell; my daughter, Christy Stowell; Lauren Ma; and Megan DeLeon for producing an incredible show and connecting us with our brilliant guests. I learned from each and every one of them.

In particular I want to acknowledge Dr. J. Stuart Ablon, Dr. Giancarlo Licata, Rick and Doris Bowman, Mikayla Caliendo, Dr. Regine Muradian, Seth Perler, Dr. Eli Lebowitz, Debra Ann Afarian, Paul Madaule, and Alexandra Dunnison whose language and ideas shared on the show found their way into my thinking as I wrote this book.

As an educator, it has always been my students who have had the greatest impact on refining my knowledge and its application in real life. I am grateful for the fun, the challenge, and the growth that they have provided. They are the true validation for the content of this book.

To my family, David, Christy, and Kevin, thank you for cheering me on in the effort to get the word out that learning disabilities and dyslexia do not have to be a stone in your shoe!

# Bibliography

Ablon, Stuart. *Changeable: How Collaborative Problem Solving Changes Lives at Home, at School, and at Work.* TarcherPerigee, 2018.

Belgau, Frank and Belgau, Beverly. *Learning Breakthrough Program.* Port Angeles, WA: Balametrics, Inc. 1982, Revised 2001.

Brandes, Bonnie M.Ed. *The Symphony of Reflexes: Interventions for Human Development, Autism, ADHD, CP, and Other Neurological Disorders.* Create Space, 2015.

Childre, Doc. *Freeze Framer.* Boulder Creek, CA: Planetary Publications, 1994.

Davis, Ronald with Braun, Eldon. *The Gift of Dyslexia.* New York, NY: Perigree Trade, 1997.

Davis, Ronald with Braun, Eldon. *The Gift of Learning.* New York, NY: The Berkley Publishing Group, 2003.

Dennison, Paul, Ph.D. and Dennison, Gail. *Brain Gym® Teacher's Edition Revised.* Ventura, CA: Edu-Kinesthetics, Inc., 1998.

Doidge, Norman. *The Brain's Way of Healing: Remarkable Discoveries and Recoveries from the Frontiers of Neuroplasticity.* USA: Penguin Books, 2016

Duffy, William. *Sugar Blues.* Grand Central Publishing, 1986.

Dweck, Carol. *Mindset-Updated Edition: Changing the Way You Think to Fulfill Your Potential.* 2017.

Farmer, Jeannette. *Train the Brain to Pay Attention the Write Way.* Denver, CO: WriteBrain Press, 1995.

Gibson, Ken, D.O. *Processing and Cognitive Enhancement* (PACE). Colorado Springs, CO: Ken Gibson, 2001

Goddard, Sally. *Reflexes, Learning, and Behavior, a Window into the Child's Mind.* Eugene, OR: Fernridge Press, 2002.

Gold, Svea. *If Kids Just Came with Instruction Sheets.* Eugene, OR: Fernridge Press, 1997.

Huberman, Andrew. Huberman Lab Podcast, 2021.

Lebowitz, Eli. *Breaking Free of Childhood Anxiety and OCD: A Scientifically Proven Program for Parents.* Oxford University Press, 2020.

Leiberman, Daniel and Long, Michael. *The Molecule of More: How a Single Chemical in Your Brain Drives Love, Sex, and Creativity and Will Determine the Fate of the Human Race.* BenBella Books, 2018.

Lindamood, Charles H. and Lindamood, Patricia C. *The A.D.D. Program: Auditory Discrimination in Depth Book 1, Understanding the Program.* U.S.A.: DLM Teaching Resources, 1979

Lyon, G. Reid and Krasnegor, Norman A. *Attention, Memory, and Executive Function.* Baltimore, MD: Paul H. Brookes Publishing Co., 2005

Perlmutter, David, MD and Coleman, Carol. *The Better Brain Book.* Riverhead Books, 2005.

Perlmutter, David, MD *Grain Brain: The Surprising Truth about Wheat, Carbs, and Sugar - Your Brain's Silent Killers.* Little, Brown Spark, 2018

Rapp, Doris, MD *Is This Your Child?* New York, NY: William Morrow and Company, Inc., 1991.

Ratey, John. MD, *A User's Guide to the Brain: Perception, Attention, and the Four Theaters of the Brain.* NY: Random House, 2002.

Ratey, John. MD, Spark: *The Revolutionary New Science of Exercise and the Brain.* Little, Brown spark, 2008.

Shaywitz, Sally. *Overcoming Dyslexia* (2020 Edition): Second Edition, Completely Revised and Updated. 2020. Vintage: (2nd Edition), 2008.

Smith, Joan, Ph.D. *Learning Victories.* Sacramento, CA: Learning Time Products, Inc., 1998.

Smith, Joan, Ph.D. *Mega Ways to Develop Executive Function*. Salinas, CA: Learning Time Products, Inc., 2019.

Smith, Joan, Ph.D. *You Don't Have to Be Dyslexic*. Sacramento, CA: Learning Time Products, Inc., 1996.

Smith, Joan, Ph.D. *Training Courses: Dyslexia Remediation Specialist Certification and EDU-Therapeutics Trainer Certification*, 1999, 2002.

Sohlberg, Johnson, Paule, Raskin, and Mateer. *APT-II Attention Process Training: A Program to Address Attention Deficits in Persons with Mild Cognitive Dysfunction*. Lash and Associates, 2002.

Sollier, Pierre. *Listening for Wellness*. Walnut Creek, CA: The Mozart Center Press, 2005.

Steinbach, Ingo. *Samonas Sound Therapy*. Keelinghusen, Germany: Techau Verlog, 1997.

Stephey, Douglas. *AMPS*. Covina, CA: Douglas Stephey, 2008.

Sunbeck, Deborah, Ph.D. *The Complete Infinity Walk; Book I: The Physical Self*. USA: The Leonardo Foundation Press, 2002.

Tomatis, Alfred, MD *The Conscious Ear*. Barrytown, NY: Station Hill Press, 1991.

Tomatis, Alfred, MD *The Ear and the Voice*. Lanham, MD: Scarecrow Press, 1997.

Truch, Stephen, Ph.D. *Discover Math*™. Calgary, AB, Canada: The Reading Foundation, 2000.

Van den Honert, Dorothy. *Wiping Out Dyslexia with Enhanced Lateralization: Musings from My Forty Years of Wiping*. AuthorHouse 2012.

## About the Author

Jill Stowell's passion for changing the lives of children and adults with dyslexia and other learning challenges led her from a small private practice to founder and executive director of Stowell Learning Centers; two time #1 Bestselling Author; program developer; and trainer and consultant for the national Fix Learning Skills network of centers for correcting learning and attention challenges.

Jill holds California teaching credentials in elementary education and learning handicaps, an MS degree in Education, a California Resource Specialist Certificate, and the Dyslexia Remediation Specialist Certification. She taught seven years in public school in mainstream, gifted, bilingual, and special education programs prior to opening the learning center.

She has trained hundreds of public and private educators in specialized learning programs, is a speaker, frequent podcast guest, and the host of the LD Expert Live broadcast and LD Expert podcast.

Jill lives with her husband in Southern California, has two wonderful adult children, and loves to bike, travel, and read.

**Also by Jill Stowell:**

"At Wits End: A Parent's Guide to Ending the Struggle Tears and Turmoil of Learning Disabilities"

"Parenting a Child with Dyslexia: Effective Practices to Help Your Child Thrive"
Rockridge Press Release Date August 16, 2022

Co-author with David Stowell: "The Dyslexia, Learning, and Attention Challenge Solution: How to Build a Profitable, Heart-Centered Business that Transforms the Learning Disability Epidemic"


Visit: www.stowellcenter.com

Podcast: www.stowelcenter.com/ldexpert

Book: www.stowellcenter.com/takethestoneout

# Index

## A

AMPS 9, 280–281, 284, 310

APT 9, 282, 284, 310

Accommodations 6, 33, 179, 184, 187, 213, 303

ADD 59–61, 70, 89, 103, 106, 108, 157, 166, 224, 257

ADHD 1–3, 5–6, 9, 54–55, 59, 70, 76, 99–100, 148–150, 246, 251, 257, 272, 275, 295, 297, 307

Advanced Brain Technologies 74, 78, 227–228, 233

Anxiety 37, 40, 53, 63, 66, 72, 74, 76, 86, 126, 143, 175, 187, 191, 222, 232, 251, 254–256, 263, 269, 287, 301, 308

Articulation 30, 83, 85, 117, 223, 242, 246

Assessment 54, 216

Asymmetrical Tonic Neck Reflex 67, 257

ATNR 67, 254, 257–259

Attention 1–3, 5–6, 9, 13, 17–18, 22–23, 25–27, 29–31, 33, 36–38, 42–45, 47–48, 51, 54–59, 63–64, 66, 68–70, 72–75, 78–79, 82–87, 89–91, 93, 95–97, 99–101, 109, 111, 115–117, 119, 124–127, 129, 132–134, 136, 145–147, 150, 153, 160–161, 165, 168, 173, 175–176, 183–186, 191, 198, 213–214, 216, 219, 225–226, 228–230, 232, 235–238, 241–242, 244, 249, 251, 253–256, 259–261, 265, 267–269, 272–274, 277, 279–287, 289, 292–293, 296, 308–310, 313–314

    Alternating Attention 279, 282

    Divided Attention 279, 282

    Selective Attention 279, 282

    Sustained Attention 279, 282

Attention Focus Training 146

Auditory Feedback Loop 8, 236–237, 248

Auditory processing 1, 3–5, 22, 29, 32–33, 44, 53, 56, 58, 70, 75, 80–89, 91, 117, 161, 169, 215, 221, 223–224, 227, 233, 235, 241, 246–247, 256–258, 261–262, 269, 287, 295

Auditory Processing Delay/Disorder 82-84, 296

Auditory Stimulation and Training 8, 58, 87, 235–236, 241, 243, 246

Auditory Zoom 8, 224–226, 233

# B

Babinski Reflex 67

Balance 5, 70, 136, 146–147, 177, 226, 231–232, 253, 255, 258, 261, 263–265, 284

BDNF 252

Bone conduction  228–229, 231, 233, 240

# C

Carbohydrates  136

Central Auditory Nervous System  226

Cognitive flexibility  97

Cognitive training  40, 106, 133, 217, 277–278, 280–282

Compensations  25, 39–40, 269, 303

Comprehension  3, 5, 7–8, 17, 22, 29, 32, 38, 42, 48, 52, 59, 70, 79–81, 83–84, 86, 89–93, 104–105, 107, 111, 113, 158, 160, 172, 181, 183, 186, 199–200, 216, 218, 223, 235–236, 238, 242–247, 259, 262, 283, 287, 292, 300, 302

Continuum  2, 44, 47–49, 51–52, 60, 64, 100, 285–286, 305

    Arousal  142, 255, 270, 285–286

Core learning skills  2, 9, 48, 58, 63, 65, 99, 219, 231, 249, 253–254, 267

Core Learning Skills Training  9, 58, 231, 253–254, 267

# D

Decoding  6, 60, 73, 106, 111, 184–185, 236, 241–243

Developmental delays  226

Differentiation  264

Doman, Alex  19, 227, 305

Dopamine  9, 128, 251, 291–292, 297

Dyscalculia  4, 7, 103, 111, 203, 258

Dysgraphia  4, 7, 103, 108–110, 191, 198, 258

Dyslexia  1–2, 4, 6, 13, 22–23, 25–26, 29–30, 37, 40, 42, 53, 59, 61, 84, 103–106, 108, 112–113, 124, 129, 133, 179, 181, 183, 186, 214, 218, 226, 238–239, 241, 248, 251, 258–259, 269, 299, 306–307, 309–311, 313–314

Dyslexia Screener  4, 113

# E

Ear infections  80, 86, 115, 226

Emotional regulation  5, 137, 198, 223, 226, 228, 250, 269, 286

Enhanced Lateralization  241, 248, 311

Executive Function  1–3, 5, 9, 48, 57, 95–98, 100–101, 153, 157–161, 165, 216, 219, 227, 269, 282, 285–289, 291–294, 301, 309–310

Exercise  9, 134, 138, 154, 159, 185, 187, 251–253, 268, 287, 309

# F

Fats  135–136

Fear Paralysis Reflex  67

Flowcharts  5, 149–150

Frequencies  8, 84, 221–226, 228–231, 236–237, 240, 270

    High Frequencies  223, 225, 231, 237, 240

    Low Frequencies  222, 225, 240

    Mid-range Frequencies  222–223, 229, 236

Sound Frequencies  8, 84, 221, 223, 226, 228–229, 236–237

# G

Graphomotor skills  191, 192, 253, 268

Grasping Reflex  67

# H

Handwriting  7, 63, 73, 109, 191–192, 195, 198, 246, 253, 257–259, 261, 266, 268

Hypotonia  226

# I

Impulse control  5, 147–148, 255, 261, 268, 274

iLs  8, 227, 229–233

Inhibitory control  97

Inner language  9, 158, 292–294

Integrated Listening Systems  8, 227, 229, 233

Intensity  8, 43, 217, 230, 268, 271, 277–278, 280–281

inTime  8, 227–228

# L

Landau Reflex  67

Language processing  17, 38, 235

Laser  70, 268, 270–271, 275

Learning disability  2, 4, 13, 26, 53–54, 115, 213, 314

Learning disabilities  13, 23, 25, 29–30, 33, 42–43, 88, 115, 124, 133, 183, 213, 225, 251, 269, 306, 314

Learning Disability Screening Tool  4, 115

Learning Skills Continuum  2, 47, 49, 51–52, 60, 64, 100, 305

Letter reversals  70, 104, 191, 262

Lindamood, Patricia  19, 33, 53, 217, 309

Listening  3, 8, 32, 73, 78–89, 91, 99, 105, 116–117, 161, 167–168, 222–233, 235–238, 241, 243–244, 246, 248, 279, 296, 310

# M

Math facts  79, 111, 123, 207

Memory  5, 7, 9, 17, 22, 31, 38, 40, 44, 48, 52, 57–58, 65, 67–68, 79, 83, 85, 91, 97, 104, 109, 111, 134–137, 145, 158, 160, 187–188, 191, 199–200, 209–210, 212, 218, 227, 229, 235, 240–241, 243–245, 251–253, 256–257, 259–262, 268, 277, 279–282, 292, 309

Metacognition  6, 9, 166, 168, 294–295

Middle ear  225–226, 232, 237, 263

Midline  68, 110, 193–195, 258–260, 262, 265–268

Moro Reflex  250, 254–256, 273

Music-Based Auditory Training  8, 221, 227

# N

Neurodevelopment  99, 216, 219, 300

Neurological Impress Reading  6, 185–186, 190, 243, 245

Neuropathways  33, 51

Neuroplastic interventions 3, 216–217

Neuroplasticity 19, 51, 142, 216, 220, 226, 233, 248, 252, 269, 275, 277, 280, 308

Neuro-timing 61, 74, 282–283

# O

Organization 5, 17, 31, 48, 58, 63, 79, 92–93, 109–112, 116, 137, 157, 167, 177, 227, 230–231, 236, 253–254, 263, 301

Organizational skills 67

# P

PACE 9, 18, 58, 61, 193, 281, 284, 299–301, 308

PATH 9, 282–283

Phonemic awareness 60, 281, 282

Phonological awareness 5, 33, 48, 52, 58, 60, 79, 83, 86, 93, 108, 117, 235, 241–242, 280

Planning 73, 92, 97, 192, 229, 253, 263, 268, 280, 285, 288, 292

Praise 1, 43, 129–130

Pre-frontal cortex 253

Primitive reflexes 56, 66, 70, 99, 250

Problem solving 2–3, 297, 307

Processing skills 3, 9, 16, 18–19, 22, 27, 30–31, 36–38, 40, 44, 48, 58, 61, 64–66, 79, 86–87, 91, 97, 99–100, 108, 119, 133, 215, 235, 241, 269, 277, 280–282, 299

Processing speed  3, 17, 22, 44, 48, 65, 79, 88–89, 277, 280–282

Psycho-educational evaluation  26

## Q

QRI  9, 250, 268–269, 271–275, 301

Quantum Reflex Integration  9, 250, 268, 301

## R

Reading  1–2, 4, 6, 8, 15–19, 22–23, 25–26, 28, 30–33, 36, 38–40, 42–43, 48, 52–53, 58–61, 67–68, 70, 72–73, 75, 79–81, 83–86, 91–93, 99, 103–107, 111, 113–114, 117, 126, 128–129, 133, 150, 172–173, 179–186, 190–191, 200, 204, 208, 212, 215–216, 218, 223, 235–236, 238–245, 248, 251, 256, 258–263, 265–267, 280–283, 296, 299–300, 311

Recorded books  183

Reflex integration  9, 249–251, 254, 268, 272, 301

Regulation  2, 5, 100, 137, 143, 176–177, 198, 222–223, 226, 228, 230, 250, 269, 278, 283, 286

Relaxation  263

Retained reflexes  2, 58, 66, 71, 272

Retention  4, 131–134, 158

Rhythm  2, 72–74, 228, 236, 245, 253, 263

## S

Safe and Sound Protocol  8, 177, 232

Screen fatigue  5, 141

Self-esteem 4, 6, 23, 28, 37, 54, 76, 129, 148, 153, 172, 174

Sensory Processing Disorder / SPD 76-78, 251

Sleep 5, 67, 137–138, 143, 175, 221, 227

Social skills 6, 32, 64, 75, 78, 83, 169, 171, 216, 223, 263

Special education 26–27, 33, 53, 213, 227, 299, 313

Speech 2, 5–6, 30–32, 70, 73–74, 80–81, 83, 85, 115, 117, 222–226, 232, 235–238, 240, 245–246, 251, 256–257, 262, 272

Spelling 4, 6, 8, 17–18, 25, 28, 31–33, 38, 40, 48, 53, 59, 61, 79, 83–85, 103, 105, 107, 109–110, 113–114, 116–117, 126, 179–181, 185–190, 197, 200, 215–216, 218, 235–236, 238, 240–243, 256–259, 262, 281, 299

Spinal Galant Reflex 56, 256–257

Spinal Perez Reflex 67

SSP 8, 232

STNR 67, 254, 259–261

Sugar 136–137, 308, 309

Symmetrical Tonic Neck Reflex 259

# T

The Listening Program 8, 78, 227

Timing 2, 61, 72–74, 245, 263, 265, 282–283

TLP 8, 78, 227, 229

TLR 69–70, 254, 261–262

Toe walking 69–70

Tomatis, Alfred 32, 224–226, 229, 233, 237–238, 310

Tonic Labyrinthine Reflex 69, 261–262

Trans-fatty acids 135

# V

Vestibular stimulation 264

Visual memory 40, 57–58, 109, 187, 200, 209, 241, 292

Visual processing 3, 16, 22, 25, 31, 44, 48, 58, 65, 72, 79, 91–93, 218, 241, 264, 281–282

Visual skills 109, 146, 254, 267

Visualization 5, 91, 158, 160, 209, 235, 241, 243, 245, 267–268, 292

# W

Working memory 44, 91, 97, 158, 229, 277, 279–280, 282

Made in United States
North Haven, CT
01 August 2022